# 35 OR MORE STRATEGIES
# FOR MY SUCCESS

By

David Christopher Platt

RoseDog Books

PITTSBURGH, PENNSYLVANIA 15238

The contents of this work, including, but not limited to, the accuracy of events, people, and places depicted; opinions expressed; permission to use previously published materials included; and any advice given or actions advocated are solely the responsibility of the author, who assumes all liability for said work and indemnifies the publisher against any claims stemming from publication of the work.

RoseDog Books
585 Alpha Drive, Suite 103
Pittsburgh, PA 15238
Visit our website at *www.rosedogbookstore.com*

**ISBN:** 978-1-63661-022-1
**eISBN:** 978-1-63661-081-8

# 35 OR MORE STRATEGIES FOR MY SUCCESS

BY: DAVID CHRISTOPHER PLATT

OCTOBER 5, 2019

Market Strategies, Business Strategies is all an entrepreneur's dream. Entrepreneurs use his or her communication skills in a fast marketplace is designed for your voice to be heard avoid missed communication or lack of interpretation. The biggest part of entrepreneurs dream is to have exquisite or exceptional listening skills and communication skills always be resourceful and helpful and have a good understanding who you are talking to, so you won't have to explain yourself Conciseness is important being Strategist or Strategic Minded by simplifying the problem or narrowing down the objectives and pinpointing in the areas that need to be fixed. Social Media and Networking such networks like Facebook, Twitter to be a part of and become as now what's know now as a social revolution other networks these are just ones that I can think of other ones such as Craigslist or eBay are some of the other ones many more to follow People use this Internet and Web as one big marketplace or one big auction that we all can see, used for advertising or marketing are product, and even who we are! and what type of person we are! can all be marketed in some way. By bringing forward there product to auction whatever they may choose for competition with others and what competitive prices or what the auction brings to them usually affordable prices that are well below cost lower after market prices they made a lot of them just as good or if not better than the ones we find in are stores we shop at or go to.

The ability to create quality strategy forms the basis of every organizational success with effectively formulated strategies being the essence of organizational profitability. Although scholars agree that the right strategy is not all that is needed for success ( implementation is also important), it's nonetheless imperative and forms the foundation of the effective management process. The strategy must, therefore, be well understood by every stakeholder in an organization since in most cases; an organization operates and is aligned around its strategies. With complexity of the global search industry, an in- depth study of google .com company's formulation process offers a conclusive understanding of the organizational strategy creation process due to its multifaceted approach of wide-ranging theoretical prescriptions. Proper analysis of Google's strategy creation offers by extension important insights on the denominators and underlying dynamics behind the contemporary global IT industry. Starting with a company summary, this paper critically assesses the strategic creation process for google.com.

Classified as one of the five most popular sites on the internet, Google.com was visited by a unique user base of over 380 million visitors in May 2008. The company was started simply as a research project by two Stanford graduate students Sergey Brin and Lawrence Page in 1996. The two sought to develop a search engine that produced a better display for search results. The domain name, Google. com was registered in 1997 and Google Inc. Incorporated on September 1998. As the world's leading search engine and one of the fastest and largest growing technology companies in the world, furthermore, it faces massive competition from companies such as Yahoo and MSN hence an analysis of how it formulates its strategies would offer further insights on what market is successful.

Google earned an estimated $3.64 billion from United States online ad revenue, an estimated 69% of all paid search- related advertising. Its market cap has overtaken that of IBM and even Chevron with an estimated value of $132 billion. It has a surplus of over $7.6 billion all of which are lacking any defined usage, has its stock a predicted to reach $600 billion by the end of this year (2008) and its one of the top ten web brands in the United States. The above summary is an indication of a model company, its success of which is attributed to its management, wide line of competitive advantages, excellent organizational control, and innovative research and development strategies. How such company formulates its strategies, in relation to the existing theoretical framework is a matter of natural interpretation.

# HOW STRATEGY IS CREATED IN GOOGLE

Google. com implements strategic planning as a deliberate process in which with the involvement of a wide range of stakeholders, top executives periodically formulate the firm's strategy. Its strategic planning process is guided by its mission that intern prescribes its objectives. Based on the objectives, the existing situation is analyzed leading to the strategy formulation, Battelle, (2005, p. 162). Based on a field review of its strategic creation process using Mintzberg's Ten Schools of Thought, the configuration school, the only one classified under the integrative category, best describes its strategic creation process for Google.com. This is because the company's strategy formation process over the years has been a transformative one. A transformative one as it has integrated the claims of other schools but at different processes in the organization, hence with a closer analysis of Google's strategy creation processes, elements of different schools of thought can be identified at different stages.

The situation analysis also forms a critical foundation of Google. com's organizational strategy. The environmental school is observable in this situation as Google has had over the years implemented a cross- section of its strategies in reaction to prevailing environmental conditions. Google analyzes its external and internal environments thereby describing its strengths, weakness in addition to existing opportunities and threats. It's through the situational analysis that large amounts of information on the company are gathered and which forms basis of strategy formulation. It's based on formulated strategies that the implementation process occurs.

## Strategic Ideas, Tools and Techniques

Research by Kostrzewa (2003, pp.62) indicates that closer analysis of the Google strategy creation process was in line with Mintzberg's second category or the process-oriented schools. The school with the most evident correlation with Google's strategy was the cognitive school. Google's strategy is formulated around the basic strategic concept of quality, customer satisfaction, and growth and has over the years served to organize the framework for the management system of the company. It has further integrated performance management system which is considered important in the alignment of its operation around its strategy. These systems have been designed during strategy design processes in an attempt to promote Google's products as unique.

Google, therefore, tries to create cognitive maps in which individuals have a global perspective of a Google world, a world exceptionally different from that created by other related companies' similar products. As listed on the companies' website, Google's operations have been guided by the philosophy of not settling for the best, Google, (2008. P. 1). Google's mission is to be a world leader in information provisions. This is to make information accessible and useful. It has displayed continued innovativeness with the introduction of multiple products into the markets. Certain products, such as Google Ad Sense were without a doubt, a success for the company, advertisers and web owners in general, Lohr, 2007. All this is based on strategy aimed at creating in potential client's minds, an aspect of real virtual reality.

The company has managed to remain competitive through multiple acquisitions of popular competitors. To present, the company has acquired more than 30 companies since its inceptions, a strategic step interpreted as creating a competitive bias toward the cultural school since most of the acquisitions have been largely popular websites on cultural domains thereby. This is advantageous to the company as it gives it more culturally inclusive appearance/ Some acquisitions of Applied Semantics Inc. which enabled them to develop an advertising campaign that earned them billions of dollars in advertising revenue to the present.

The 2006 acquisition of writely, an online processing firm led to the development of Google does witch since its inception in 2006, has seen a rise in its revenue. Google further acquired YouTube, in 2006 for a record $1.6 billion which has seen it dominate the online video industry. All the listed acquisitions in addition to its renowned status as a world leading free provider of search engine have provided Google with a platform for creating an impression of a collective and cooperative organization, hence the support of the cultural school in its strategy formulation.

Although individuals' approaches can be identified in Google's strategy creation processes, a rather integrative approach, combining several approaches have been Google's key success secrets as it has managed to constantly transform it by subscribing to ideal strategic and timely changes. The company has made efforts to acquire competitors in a bid to remain competitive in the global IT market an example is 2007 acquisition of double click, an advertising competitor for a record $3.1 billion. It also acquired tonic systems which enabled it to acquire the capacity to convert Microsoft PowerPoint files into HTML and PDF documents. This boosted its competition with Microsoft which had gained a considerable market base based on its Microsoft Office product. Furthermore, this integrative a constantly changing approach can be viewed in Google ability to offer a wide range of products a reflection of its technologically sound and alert team of innovators. Continuous intensive research is undertaken in the Google laboratories, online text locations or in the Google.com website itself. Products are generally of high quality and utility.

Google strategic priority is the integration of desktop and internet search, yet its biggest competitor is Yahoo followed by Microsoft, Ask.com and American Online respectively through on the variety of Google's products and services, it is difficult to exactly determine its competitors. Yahoo provides similar products such as e- mail services, maps, financial analysis, of Google. Google's strategy to provide unique services thereby attracting specific clique of individuals has largely paid off.

For example, comparing Microsoft to Google, Microsoft offers to search and other few online services similar to those offered by Google through the main lines of business is the design and sales of software and operating systems. Competition comes into focus due to the recent launch of Google Docs & Spreadsheets and Google Gears, presentation software that challenges the dominance of Microsoft Windows. In term of sales, products and geographical distribution, Google accounts for over 50%, Yahoo, Microsoft, Ask.com and AOL each have an estimated market share of 28.5%, 10%, 5%, and 4% respectively, Khaki- Sedigh & Roudaki, (2003).

Elements of the Entrepreneurial school are also observable on Google's organizational strategy. AA considerable proportion of the company's control has also been governed by the solid executive control with the focus being given to chief managers led by the top executives. There has been the rewarding of the well -performing management team since 2002 with the managers who are underperforming being demoted or reshuffled sense of a general focus on management. The organization has also adopted the clan control mechanism. Although Google's employees have many things in common the company has continuously emphasized visionary leadership.

They share many values, expectations and goals hence tend to work in harmony with one another; a harmony created by the aspects of strong visionary leadership. This has been displayed in the less formal approach in which the google team approaches issues. The integrated approach used by Google has ensured grater cost savings, increased efficiency, better product quality, enhanced customer service and a happier cohesive workforce who work in harmony to produce positive results; hence although its strategy is based on cognitive school, the entrepreneurial school is certainly considerably evident on its strategy formulation process.

The company has had a rather integrated approach to achieving in its strategy formulation process; applying both bureaucratic, market and clan control mechanisms. Google has a board of governors and a core management team together with specialized well-documented rules and regulations implemented through a formal authority that serve to guide employee performances. This bureaucratic type of approach has been applied mildly and served to regulate Google employee's behavior thereby leading to better results, limited budgets, better performances as displayed in statistical reports and employee performance records.

Google was ranked the best company to work for in 2006 survey by the fortune magazine in 2007, fortune, (2007p. 1). The assertion of power school is therefore evident in Google strategic formulation as the company has managed to properly manage its employees. It has succeeded in creating a generally goo working environment for all its employee though some critics see this as making them loose a considerable proportion of daily tasks. It has been characterized by offering its employees a large degree of freedom thereby tapping their creativity towards the improvement of both its products and services. Hence the assertion of the power school is evident in its strategy formulation.

According to Battelle, (2006, p.99). Google's strategies have been guided by its desire to increase profitability through the increment of sales while maintaining or reducing the costs goods sold. Estimates show that Google's net income grew from $100 million in 2002 to $3,077 billion in 2005. Its cost of goods sold was generally constant being maintained at approximately 40% of sales. On common basc analysis, Google had 2,412 % increase in sales in the five-year period between 2002 and 2006 with a net income increment of over 3,088% within the same period, Battelle, (2006, p.99).

This effective strategy formulation process has resulted in considerable cash surplus resulting from balances in short and long -term investments. Google has neither short nor long term debt through IPO offered an increase in capital surplus in 2004. With the continued rise in its share prices, Google's capital surplus has continued to rise over the years furthermore being a service- oriented company. Google has no looming inventory. On the basis of ratio analysis, Google's sales increased from 1.2 in 2002 to 29.05 in 2006. Over the past five years, Google has had more money at hand than they know what to do with, an attribute that has been seen on its rather many strategic acquisitions furthermore Google's profit margin fluctuated between 2002 and 2003 but increased steadily to an estimated 60.2 % in 2006, an aspect attributable to its effective strategy formulation process, Johnson, Scholes, Whittington, (2008,p.4).

Driven by large revenues from advertisement, Google. com has invested massively in its Research and Development Budget. Its research findings are a critical component of its strategic formulation process. Varied sections of google have had different approaches to attaining solutions to various world problems such as new technological advancement, pharmaceutical research, and online advertisements, Pringle, Allison & Dowe, (1998, p. 379). Google has invested massively in research and development though it was not classified under the top ten R&D spenders until 2007. This followed from massive increments in the company's spending on Research and Development when spending increased by over 73% to a record – breaking $2.1 billion in the year 2007 compared to the budget in 2006. Since 2007, it is estimated that Google's R&D spending has stayed above 13 % of its total revenue which is a representation of more than double the amount spent prior to the year 2002. Massive research is being undertaken on how Google can enter into other business projects such as Android, TV Ads, and other projects to further boost its growth.

**Summary and Conclusion.**

As a result of its advanced strategy formulation process, its better display of search results, the simple approach that was incorporated in the searching process, Google has grown in popularity and acceptance the world over. Presently, the company employees are in excess of 10,000 people from all continents of the world. It is the largest company offering search- related advertising yet Search Related advertisement is fastest growing of all the online ad businesses with an estimated annual growth rate at 41%. Pringle, Allison & Dowe, (1998, p. 378)

Although Google's strategy creation results from consultation of a wide-ranging stakeholders in the organization, stringent rules aimed at protecting some of its products and services are still prescribed by its top management. For example, in 2005 the top management introduced a trend that required all Ad sense members to sign a gagging clause. The clause has restricted web owners from unfairly benefiting from the proceeds gained from advertising, Google has been continuously innovative, being innovated and the first to implement its strategies. For example, it was the first company to implement the Ad Relevance Strategy, a strategy that ensured it provided broad matching on all search terms. It further went ahead to set a system in which a single price was set on all ads, Moran & Hunt, (2006, p. 22).

Conclusively, although the execution is more important, good vision in the creation of effective strategies are the primary essentials to management success. The strategy should be understood and interpreted in terms that are understandable and that can be acted upon. With a strong reputation and familiarity, good speed in its search procedures, user - friendliness in its product output, relevance in ranking of its research results together with technologically advanced additional services witch are multidisciplinary in nature, available multiple opportunities seen in the ever- increasing online advertisement, higher usage volubility as it gains more customer base across the global domain, and the introduction of new products, Google will surely continue to dominate the market for certain undefined periods of time. Definitely, Google Inc. has been a role model to technological businesses and still has great potential as a company.

# APPEARANCE.

We take selective and making good personal judgements and status queue, interpersonal personas, and interpretations of people e-tier and the way they Carrie there selves is important for someone's success resulting in instant judgement-laced labels: The meeting was a waste of time, your tie is to wide, your designer sun- glasses don't look good on you they look better on them.

So, feedback givers rarely share the raw observations behind their labels because they simply aren't aware of them. It's up to you to help them sort it out. Your goal here is not to ignore or dismiss the interpretation. Data is crucial, but so is the interpretation. At the very least, it's one-person view of things. So, you want to get a clear picture of both data and interpretation.

Not all feedback has a forward- looking component. You notice that your tennis partner has trouble remembering the score. If you share that observation with their spouse, you may not have any advice that goes along with that. You might- "here are three behavioral changes to watch for that may signal for dementia"- but it also could be that your purpose is achieved just by sharing the observation with you spouse or someone else.

Often through, feedback will have forward looking components. As we'll see below, with coaching, that piece is about advice; with evaluation, it's about consequences and expectations.

In any given case, you might or might not choose to follow someone's advice. But we can test whether advice is clear by asking this. If you do want to follow the advice, would you know how to do so?

Too often the answer is no, because the advice that they have not reassuring enough, not enough information, simply too vague. "If you want to shine at work make yourself indispensable."

Biases Drive Data Collection.

There's another factor that makes difference spotting tough. What we do and don't notice isn't random. If your giver likes you and thinks your terrifically competent, they're going to notice all the fantastic things you do. They'll go out of their way to find them. Your radiance also influence how they interpret what they see. That mistake you made is simply the exception that proves just how competent you usually are, and maybe it wasn't really a mistake at all.

But the friction develops in the relationship- when the infatuation of new loves fades, the stakes rise, or humidity sets in- biases shift. Now your giver begins to focus on the things you have messed up while ignoring those you got right. Your willingness to take risk" is now seen as risky," your firm hand on the tiller" is now regarded as an unwillingness to let go. Others seek data that confirm their preexisting view of us, whether that view is good or bad. It's human nature.

Meanwhile, we have biases of our own. All things being equal, we'll find a sympathetic story that explains and justifies our own behavior. We remember what we got right, and as we'll explore in the next chapter, we ascribe generally good intentions to ourselves. Ninety-three percent of American motorist believe they are better than average drivers. In a 2007 Business week poll, 90 percent of the managers surveyed believed their performance in the workplace to be in the top 10 percent.

These biases can make a difference spotting tougher still since we each feel it's the other who is biased. In fact, were both biased, and we each need the other in order to see the whole picture more clearly.

E-mail Body Language.

Surprisingly, even on e-mail, people try to read emotions and tone. Or more precisely, despite lacking access to the sender's face and voice, we retain the desire to know their mood and what their real intentions, so we gather what we do know about it such as clues and different body languages.

E-mail can provide obvious clues, like All Caps, lot of people with answers to the questions but are any of them the right answer, and who is suddenly (strategically?) cc'ed as well as more subtle ones like word choice or timing. We wonder why they responded instantly, or why they waited so long. Was their three- word response pointed or merely to the point? Was their outpouring of words just thorough, or a sign of exasperation? We know what they said; we want to know what they meant.

Douglas Stone and Sheila Heen ,Thanks for the feedback: the science and art of receiving feedback well even when it is off base, unfair poorly delivered, and frankly, you're not in the mood pg.56 par.1 pg.57par.3 pg.63 par.4 pg.64 pg.85 par.1).

# HEALTH

The low-fat craze from the mid-1990s is responsible for today's conventional wisdom that anything with fat is bad for you. A lot of people- especially weight conscious teenage girls- have been taught hate having any food with fat. Sure, eating the wrong fat adds pounds to your midsection, clogs your arteries, and puts you at risk for developing cancer, but eating to little is just as deadly. Since the Israelites were instructed to eat the fat of the land, so to speak, why didn't they create know saturated fats and cholesterol are the main causes of coronary disease and malignancies?

Actually, and to no surprise, the opposite is true. By giving us these healthy animal fats, God in His infinite wisdom provided us a concentrated source of energy, and these very fats are the source material for cell membranes and various hormones. Without fats providing satiety, we would be hungry with-in minutes of finishing a meal, who would have thought that fats were so important- or good for you?

But you have to eat the right fats- foods loaded with omega-3 polyunsaturated fats and monounsaturated (omega-9) fatty acids, as well as healthy saturated fats. These good fats are found in a wide rang of foods, including salmon, lamb, and goat meet, goat's and sheep's milk and cheese, walnuts and olives. It's also better to eat butter- yes old school butter – than margarine, which is manmade, chemically altered fat. The Medical Research Council found that men eating butter ran half the risk of developing heart disease as those eating margarine.

I addition, Greeks, Austrians, and the swiss are known for their high- fat diets (lots of butter and cheese), but they rank in the top half- dozen countries for longevity. And much has been made about the French, who never meet a cream dish they didn't like. A French woman, Mireille Guiliano, topped the book charts with French Women Don't Get Fat: The Secret Eating for Pleasure. A book about how to have your cake and eat it too.

Fats rich in omega-3 and saturated fats such as medium- chain and short- chain fatty acids play a crucial role in the body chemistry. Sally Fall ion points out that saturated fatty acids, constitute at least 50 percent of the cell membranes, play vital role in health for are bones, enhance the immune system, protect the liver from alcohol and other toxins, and guard against harmful microorganisms in the digestive track.

Not all fats Hydrogenated fats are found in practically every are good for you, and I want to make that clear. You want to steer away from Hydrogenated fats, which have been cancer. processed food, from triscuits to Wonder Bread, from Twinkies to Skippy peanut butter. Most of the oils used in the households today-soybean, safflower, cottonseed, and corn- are partially hydronated oil, witch by definition, are liquid fats that have been injected with hydrogen gas at high temperatures under high pressure to make associated with a host of maladies, including diabetes, obesity, and them solid at room temperature.

I urge you to cook with butter or extra- virgin coconut oil was the "go -to" oil of it's day until cooking oil manufactures found a way to produce their products cheaper and push coconut oil off the store shelves. That's to bad because foods cooked in coconut oil taste great. Coconut oil is packed with antioxidants and reduces the bod's need for vitamin E. You can tell which oil is better just by comparing how fast real canola oil or salt flower oil becomes rancid when sitting at room temperature. Coconut oil shows no signs of rancidity even after a year at room temperature.

The reason I tell you this is that after my health improved and I resumed a normal life, I continued to seek out supplements made with soil base organisms and other probiotic microorganisms witch are known in the natural health industry as "Whole Food" or "living" multivitamins. I was convinced that the nutrients produced a probiotic fermentation- a process in which beneficial bacteria and yeast are created into beneficial compounds, that enhance digestive and immune system health- are a missing link to good health. These probiotics contained many different compounds, such as organic acids, antioxidants, and key nutrients that were essential to human's health. Beneficial microorganisms found in the soil and on plants are also played a key role in Biological transmutation, which is scientific jargon for evidence of nonradioactive, low- energy transmutation of light elements in plants, animals. And minerals.

I also studied the work of Dr. Weston Price, a Cleveland dentist who lived from 1870 to 1948. As he filled more and more cavities of patients sitting in his dental chair, he wondered, "could it be our processed foods?" Dr. Price left his practice and traveled around the world studying indigenous people whose teeth and gums were untouched by processed foods. He came into contact with fourteen primitive cultures who not only displayed row after row of healthy teeth, but these smiling men, and women and children also lived healthy lives virtually free of physical disease. When Dr. Price wrote his findings, he was convinced that the American standard diet- sad- was sending us down the road to perdition. Clearly a man ahead of his time, Dr. Price posited that restoring nutrients-dense foods into our diets would do us a world of good.

When I examined Dr. Price's writings, I paid close attention to the type and form of the nutrients contained in foods- meats, dairy, fruits, vegetables, botanicals, sea vegetables, and mushrooms- that the worlds happiest people consumed. That gave me a baseline to search for a "living" multivitamin that was the sum of nature's richest sources of these key nutrients. Although I couldn't go back to the lifestyles of our ancestors, I would certainly ingest nutrients in the forms they and get at least part of the way there. My goal was to find a multivitamin that was close to food as possible, which complies with the second criterion of eating- eat food in a form that is healthy for the body.

That's why I highly recommend that you take living multivitamins in whole food form, also known as homeostatic nutrients, witch are vitamins and minerals that have been fermented with probiotic microorganisms and their enzymes.(you'll find a list of such products in the GRX Resource Guide.) Basically the nutrient complexes that make up the multivitamins have been put through a fermentation process (similar to the digestive process of the body) that takes isolated nutrients and recombines them in a form found in food so the body can recognize it and utilize it better.

These multivitamins also contain a broad array of antioxidants from fruits, vegetables, herbs, and spices. Antioxidants are compounds that preserve and protect other compounds in the body from free radical damage. Without going into long explanations, free radicals are something you don't want to run rampant within your molecular system. Free radicals are oxygen molecules with a single electron, but these unstable molecules are known to attack the immune system's cells. Antioxidants neutralize free radicals, which is a good thing.

The most well- known antioxidant are vitamin E and C and Beta - Carotene. Though scientific research, we've learned that vitamin E is a fat-soluble vitamin present in nuts, seeds, whole grains, apricots, vegetables, and eggs laid by healthy chickens. Vitamin C, chemically known as ascorbic acid, is water- soluble vitamin present in green peppers, cabbage, spinach, broccoli, kale, cantaloupe, kiwi, strawberries, and citrus fruits and their juices. Beta-carotene is a precursor to vitamin A (which means the body converts beta- carotene to vitamin A) and is present in butter from grass feed cows, spinach, carrots, cereal grasses such as wheat and barley, squash, broccoli, yams, tomatoes, cantaloupes, and peaches.

Take another look at those foods I just described. Do you think the average person is eating enough of those foods to receive the antioxidants he or she needs? Does a typical American diet of a Danish and coffee for breakfast, hamburger and French fries for lunch, and spaghetti and meatballs with garlic bread for dinner fit this bill?

I don't think so, which is why I think everyone needs to take a living multivitamin daily- even folks who eat as healthy as I do. We all need a boost that only a living multivitamin can deliver.

(Cite: The Great Physician Rx for health and wellness/Jordin Rubin with David Remedios pg. 21 par.2- pg. 22).

# COD LIVER OIL

Another supplement that I universally recommend is the underappreciated cod- liver oil.

You may be thinking, you mean that horrible- tasting stuff they gave to me when I was in labor for hours and the baby wouldn't come out?

No, that would be castor oil. Code-live oil, on the other hand, contains four nutrients that hardly any of us get enough of. These four nutrients are eicosatetraenoic acid (EPA), docosahexaenoic acid (DHA), vitamin A, and vitamin D.

EPA and DHA are long -chain polyunsaturated fats known as omega-3 fatty acids, which are found in cold water fish and eggs from chickens that run around and eat worms. Omega- 3 is also present in flaxseed oil, hemp seed oil, and pumpkin seed oil, although it occurs as alpha linolenic acid, which must be converted by the body into EPA and DHA.

But EPA and DHA are best found in cold water fish, especially the golden oils extracted from the filleted livers of Icelandic cod. This rich source of valuable nutrients began showing up in the fishing communities of Norway, Scotland, and Iceland in the middle of the nineteenth century as people discovered the health benefits of cod- liver oil. They endured harsh winters with long periods of darkness in some of the most remote places in the world, so whenever someone came off a fishing boat sneezing up a storm, he couldn't run down to Wal-Mart for some Sudafed or Nyquil.

Instead, they turned to cod- liver oil because they had learned over the years that its medicinal properties were a natural, effective remedy for many of the infections that allied them. By the 1890s, cod- liver oil was commonly used rickets and malnourished children, and adults relied upon it when they complained of rheumatism or arthritis. People in the old days believed cod- liver oil "lubricated the joints."

Cod- liver oil became popular in this country at the turn of the twentieth century, and I'm sure your parents or grandparents haven't forgotten the time when they held their noses while the patient administered a teaspoon of the fishy smelling liquid. For a long time, however cod- liver oil had a reputation as a vile substance. Apprehensive mothers often resorted to a "spoonful of sugar to make the medicine go down," as Mary Poppins used to sing. When improvements in the extraction and preparation of cod- liver oil occurred, progress was made in how it smelled and tasted. These days, cod- liver oil comes in lemon, mint, and other flavors that mask the fishy odor and taste. I'll admit cod-liver oil is an acquired taste. But after a week or two, you'll get used to swallowing a spoonful.

I added cod- liver oil to my daily diet nearly ten years ago during my recovery from illness, and now I'm to the point where I can drink the stuff right out of a bottle. That's nothing, though, compared to the Hotel Borg in Reykjavik, Iceland, where they serve cod- liver oil in cordial glasses during breakfast!

These days, Icelandic schools have made cod- liver oil a lunch time staple because of lack of sunshine in the winter and their recognition that the vitamin D in cod- liver oil builds strong bones and keeps rickets at bay. If schoolkids in Reykjavik can handle cod- liver oil, you can too. I recommend that you place this enduring, time- proven nutritional gem on your list of supplements and begin taking between one teaspoon and one tablespoon a day. Cod- liver oil helps prevent bone deterioration in adults, improves cardiovascular function, and contributes to long life. Life insurance data and genetic research have shown that Icelandic people are medical marvels, displaying less heart disease and high blood pressure than most people in other cultures of the world.

Your children should be taking cod-liver oil, too, because the fatty acids in cod- liver oil are important for the development of the brain and the nervous system. Cod- liver oil helps concentration. David Horrobin, a medical and biochemical researcher, once told me, "If you want to prevent learning disabilities in your children, feed them cod- liver oil." The omega- 3 fatty acids presented in cod- liver oil is not only wonderful for your immune system, but for your skin and health as well. The high levels of vitamin D are especially helpful if you're very careful about the amount of sunlight you expose yourself to.

Cod- liver oil contains more vitamin A per unit weight than any other common foods- almost three times more than beef liver, the next richest source. Most people are deficient in vitamin A because they don't regularly eat beef livers or butter produced from cows fed only grass from irrigated fields year-round. Vitamin A is not found in carrots or greens, despite what you may have heard; that beta carotene, which can be converted into vitamin A by a healthy liver.

Vitamin A is extremely important to the health and integrity of the mucosal linings of the body, such as gastrointestinal tract and the lungs. When you have a virus or flu, however, your body gets depleted of vitamin A, which is another reason to sip on a teaspoon of cod- liver oil each evening.

Cod liver oil - it doesn't get a lot of respect. But study after study shows that people who use cod liver oil are less likely to develop multiple sclerosis, arthritis, or coronary heart disease. And check this: a study of Norwegian women showed that women who consumed cod- liver oil is one of the best- selling supplements in Europe, and it should be the same on this side of the Atlantic Ocean.

# GREEN SUPERFOODS

The average American consumes less than the recommended three-to- five servings a day of "greens," and the most beneficial are the deep green, leafy vegetables. In fact, Americans eat way less than they should when it comes to consuming their green veggies. The United States Department of Agriculture estimates more than 90 percent of the population fail to eat five to nine servings of fruits and vegetables daily, which are some of the most beneficial foods that god created on this planet.

This amazes me in our land of plenty. Here we are, living in a blessed nation where fruits and vegetable are readily available at market and roadside stands, and people don't avail themselves of these natural foods that are so good for us. Thanks to modern transportation and shipping methods, we can shop all year round: fuji apples from Chile, ruby red strawberries from New Zeeland, Has avocados from Mexico, and fresh lettuce and tomatoes from our nation's breadbasket every month of the year. Do we eat enough of them? No.

I wonder what those Icelandic fishing families of yesteryear, who would have jumped at joy at the chance to eat a harvest salad in the dead of winter, would think of us now- a culture to apathetic to stock our refrigerators with fresh fruits and vegetables, it just goes to show you the wisdom of Solomon, who wrote: "Some people are so lazy that they won't even lift a finger to feed themselves" (Prov.19:24NLT). The ancient king must have known that our culture would squander one of the most powerful weapons against potent diseases. Fruits and vegetables when consumed optimal amounts, have been shown in countless studies to protect us against the ravages of heart disease, high blood pressure, cancer, diabetes, and almost every killer disease common to modern men and women.

Besides not eating a lot of green leafy vegetables, we don't eat grass, yes, I said grass, and I'm not talking about the type

you smoke, I'm referring to barley grass, wheat grass, oat grass and alfalfa grass, witch are commonly known cereal grasses. Barley grass has been a part of a healthy diet since biblical times, mainly because barley was the first green plant to spout up through the earth after a long winter. The Egyptians, Israelites, Greeks, and Romans made young barley sprouts a dietary staple. I mentioned earlier in the chapter that wheat and barley grasses were promoted in the 1930s as one of the first multivitamins.

Cereal grasses contain a broad array of enzymes, vitamins, minerals, proteins, and chlorophyll, which is the greener pigment as found in plants. Chlorophyll makes life on earth possible because the oxygen we breath comes from the chlorophyll rich green plants. Our human blood is identical to chlorophyll with one exception the main elements in the blood is iron, while the main element in chlorophyll is magnesium. Nothing matches the nutritive density found in barley or other grasses such as wheat, rye, corn, rice, oats, sorghum, miller, and spelt.

In the 1930s and 1940s, American's leading scientists, led by agriculture biochemists George Kohler, embarked on grass research at the University of Wisconsin. They compared the growth of guinea pig fed one of four foods dried grass powder, lettuce, cabbage, and spinach, the guinea pigs fed dried grass powder thrived and gained normal weight, those that ate lettuce, cabbage, or spinach lost or barely sustained their weight.

Charles Schnabel, another agricultural biochemist, carried out similar experiments with chickens. Those fed cereal grass increased winter egg production by 94 percent and produced stronger, healthier chicks. Credit was given to the blood-building ability of grasses like wheat grass and barley, thanks to the presence of chlorophyll, witch the body transforms into hemoglobin, thereby increasing the red blood cell count and the blood's capacity to deliver oxygen and other nutrients to the cells of the body.

As I learned of the importance of whole food nutrition, I saw the value of taking a "green food" supplement that was a certified organic blend of barley, wheat, oat, and alfalfa grass juices combined with other vegetables, tart fruits, microalgae such as spirulina and chlorella, and sprouted grains and seeds. Once I began blending a couple scoops of green foods "superfoods." And while the taste didn't thrill me at first, after regular use, my body actually began to crave it. For those who can't stomach the thought of drinking their greens, you've got no more excuses, because high-quality are now available in caplets.

A combination of green superfood product is a "must have" for your daily regime. (A list of recommended green superfoods supplements can be found in the GPRx resource guide, page 347.) A nutritious green superfood powder combines the dietary benefits of whole food living nutrients and often contain whole food fiber sources, and green food powders mix well with water on your favorite fruit or vegetable juice, If your looking for nutrition on the go before you leave the house for work in the morning, a glass of green super food powder in water or juice provides convenient nutrition. Green foods also do wonders for keeping regular.

Final thoughts about green superfood blends: the nutritional content in a high- quality green food powder often has grater amounts of various nutrients, such as vitamin A, riboflavin, folic acid, magnesium, and calcium than single servings of fresh, raw garden vegetables like broccoli, cabbage, carrots, cauliflower, cucumber, lettuce, spinach, and tomatoes. How is this done?

The answer is in juicing, low-temperature drying, and fermentation-nature's way of preparing foods for easy assimilation into the human body. The fermentation of foods is accomplished by beneficial microorganisms, producing enzymes and organic acids that breakdown foods into their most usable compounds. You should seek out green food manufacturers that use a fermentation process to make their product. Some companies- like those that produce multivitamins- use fillers since it's an expensive process to transform thirty pounds of wheat and barley grass juices, for example, into a pound of green food powder. If you see ingredients like apple fiber, lecithin, chicory, or inulin on the ingredient label, that's a strong sign that green food has been diluted by filler ingredients, making it not nearly as beneficial to you.

As the old Joni Mitchell song from the Sixties goes, we need to "get Back to the garden"

Eat your green foods.

# WHOLE FOOD FIBER

When searching for a fiber product that's right for you, choose a brand that was made from organic seeds, grains, and legumes that are fermented or sprouted for ease of digestion. One of the best ways to consume whole food fiber is to take it first thing in the morning and just before bed. Just mix it with your green superfood powder, and you've given your body more nutrition than most people get in a week. (For a list of recommended whole food fiber products, see the GPRx Resource Guide, page 347).

# PROBIOTICS

Most people, when they see their family physician for a sinus problem or a nasty bronchitis infection, walk out of doctor's office holding a prescription for antibiotics. Medically speaking, antibiotics are a variety of natural or synthetic substances that inhibit the growth of- or destroy-microorganisms.

Since their discovery in the 1930s, antibiotics have made it possible to cure bacteria- related disease such as pneumonia, tuberculosis, and meningitis. So, if antibiotics are supposed to be good for us, what about probiotics? Does that mean there bad for us.

Just the opposite, I can assure you. By definition, probiotics are living, direct-fed microbials (DFMs) that promote growth of beneficial bacteria in the intestines. In fact, I would argue that the lack of probiotics in our diets can be associated with a whole array of intestinal problems like aforementioned Crohn's disease, gastritis, and ulcerative colitis, along with high cholesterol levels, allergies, skin conditions, frequent colds, and the flu. Our society has developed into an antibiotic culture so intent on destroying bacteria that we've eradicated much of the beneficial bacteria in our bodies and the environment, thanks to the development of antibiotic drugs, the introduction chlorinated water, the onset of air pollution, and continued reliance on a poor diet.

After I recover from my intestinal disorders with the help of beneficial microorganisms from food and supplement. For Instance, I learned that the normal human gastrointestinal tract contains hundreds of different species of harmless bacteria, otherwise known as intestinal flora. When the normal balance of these bacteria is disturbed by illness or antibiotic treatment, an imbalance occurs, and the result is often constipation or diarrhea.

Probiotics I learned worked by colonizing the intestinal tract and crowding out disease- causing bacteria, viruses, and yeast.

Probiotics are available in two formats: food dietary supplements. Unfortunately, we've been sterilizing our soil for the last fifty to one hundred years with pesticides and herbicides, destroying good and bad bacteria. An easy place to find foods containing probiotic bacteria is your grocery store dairy case, where you can reach for probiotic- rich yogurt, kefir, or raw sauerkraut.

Dietary supplements are a great way to reintroduce beneficial microorganisms into your digestive tract, which can improve bowel and immune system function, increase nutrient absorption, and detoxify the body and its organs. I think the best probiotics are the ones that contain soil -based organisms (SBOs), which are room -temperature stable and do not require refrigeration as most common probiotic supplements do.

In the old days, before farmers called in crop dusters to spray their fields with pesticides, our soils teemed with microorganisms, many of which were beneficial to our digestive tracts and immune system. I've seen clinical studies showing that people with Crohn's disease, irritable bowel syndrome, constipation, candida, asthma, and other allergies demonstrated dramatic changes in health once they added probiotics to their supplement plan.

# DIGESTIVE ENZYMES

I mentioned that I stock digestive Enzymes in my silver supplements case, and I always make sure I take a couple before I dig into a restaurant meal. Let me explain why: when we eat raw foods, such as salad and fruit, we consume the enzymes they contain. When we eat cooked or processed meals, like in a restaurant, however, the body's pancreas must produce the enzymes necessary to digest them. The constant demand for enzymes strains the pancreas, which must kick in more enzymes to keep up demand. Without the proper levels of enzymes from foods- either raw or fermented- or from taking supplements, you are susceptible to excessive gas and bloating, diarrhea, constipation, heartburn, and low energy.

Digestive enzymes are complex proteins involved in the digestive process. They are the body's day laborers, the ones responsible for synthesizing, delivering, and eliminating the unbelievable number of ingredients and chemicals that your body uses during the waking hours. When the body produces enzymes, their job is to stimulate chemical changes in the food passing through the gut. The pancreas, which takes the lead role in producing digestive enzymes for the body, has to keep up by producing pancreatic enzymes. Those with pancreatic problems such as cystic fibrosis usually require some form of digestive enzyme, but junk- food diets, fast chewing, and eating on the run contribute to the body's inability to produce adequate enzyme production and the subsequent malabsorption of food, These problems get worse as we age not better.

A leading biochemist, Dr. Edward Howell, cited numerous animal studies in his book Enzyme Nutrition, showing that animal fed diets deficient in enzymes experienced enlargement of the pancreas because the organ was working overtime to produce digestive enzymes. It wasn't long before their health was severely affected. One could eat more raw food in its natural, unprocessed state, but that isn't always possible, as I can attest when I travel or have a heavy social schedule. The last thing you want to eat when you have these types of digestive problems is fried foods because items like fried chicken and French fries must be cooked in oil at high temperatures than the boiling point, witch damages fats and destroys enzymes.

So, if you're having trouble finding a way to eat enough raw, fresh, live foods like bananas, avocados, seeds, nuts, grapes, and other natural foods, then take plant- based digestive enzymes to ease the digestion of the food. Digestive enzymes are available at your local natural food store and can find recommended brands in the GPRx resource Guide, page 348.

The Great Physician Rx for Health and Wellness/ Jordin Rubin with David Remedios pg.82 par.6 – pg. 94

# HYGIENE

To protect others, as well as yourself, it's vital to keep your hands sanitary and clean as people will respect you for the type of person you are, and they will then begin to have relations or develop a bond with you. This will generates into your only as good as you feel, if you feel like a clean person you usually feel clean about yourself, and is positive for good business, and is positive for good one on one communication with people, You begin by incorporating the three elements of hand washing: soap, running water, and friction, although I would add a fourth- motivation. There's no excuse why anyone should neglect washing his/her hands after going to the bathroom, handling meat, or touching doors and other property in public places. A few seconds at the sink can save you hours or even days of discomfort or a trip to the doctor's office.

When it comes to steering clear of germs, I exercise common sense and practice advanced hygiene. For instance, I've done dozens of book signings in the last year, and at these appearances, I usually shake hands with a couple of hundred people. While I'm happy to greet new people in this manner, the moment the book signing is over, I return to my hotel room and wash my hands thoroughly by digging them into semisoft soap to remove germs from underneath my fingernails. Then I lather the soap over my cuticles for fifteen seconds and rinse with running water as warm as I can stand.

From the hands and fingernails, germs can enter the body through the nasal passageway or the corner of the eyes- the tear ducts- when we touch those areas. All of us rub our faces so often that we don't even know we're doing it half the time, but when skin-on-skin or skin-on-membrane contact is made, we transfer a lot of different variety's of bacteria, allergens, environmental toxins, and viruses from one part of the body to another. In medical terms, it's called auto- or self- inoculation of the conjunctival (the eyes) or nasal mucosa (the nose) with a single finger.

Hand- to- face contact happens dozens, if not hundreds, of times a day. The next time you're sitting in a meeting, trying to stay awake, take a look around. How often does Betty in accounting touch her nose? What about Jeremy from IT? How often is he rubbing his eyes and mouth? And what about those times you pass somebody on the freeway, and you notice the driver doing some "nasal maintenance"?

The areas underneath the fingernails, around the membranes of the eyes, and the membranes of the eyes, and the membranes in the front part of the nasal passageway areas to keep clean. I follow a five- step advanced hygiene system at home and on the road. The system is based on research done by Australian scientist Kenneth Seaton, Ph.D., who discovered that ear nose and throat problems- which represent 80 percent of visits to doctor's offices – were linked to the fact that humans inoculate there noses, eyes, mouths, and skin with dirty fingernails throughout the day.

So always remember the practices of clean hygiene consists of:

Wet your hands with warm water. It doesn't have to be anywhere near scalding hot.

Apply plenty of soap to palms of both hands. The best soap to use is a semisoft soap that you can dig your fingernail into (see GPRx Resource Guide, page 349, for advanced hygiene products)

Rub your hands vigorously together and scrub all the surfaces. Pay attention to the skin between the fingers and work the soap into the fingernails.

Rub and scrub for fifteen to thirty seconds, or about the time it takes to slowly sing "Happy Birthday to Me."

Rinse well and dry your hands on a paper towel or clean cloth towel. If you're in a public restroom, it's a good idea to turn off running water with the towel in your hand. An even better idea is to use that same towel to open that door since the door handle is the first place that non-washers touch after they go to the bathroom.

Keep waterless sanitizers in your purse or wallet in case soap and water are not available in public restroom. These towelettes, although not ideal, are better than nothing.

When to Wash Your Hands:
- After you go to the bathroom
- Before and after you insert and remove contact lenses
- Before and after food preparation
- Before you eat
- After you sneeze, cough, or blow your nose
- After cleaning up after your pet
- After handling money
- After changing a diaper
- After blowing a child's nose
- After handling garbage
- After cleaning toilets
- After shaking hands with a bunch of people
- After shopping at the supermarket
- After attending an event at a public theater
- Before and after sexual intercourse

The Great Physician Rx for Health and Wellness/ Jordin Rubin With David Remedios Pg.112 par.6-pg.113 pg.115, pg.118

# GENUINE.

To strategically acclimated and be a force reckoned for, and to be very successful person it's the way that you apply yourself and handle situations and integrate respectfully with other people to be success these are strategy's that are helpful for people to be successful. And be the successful people that they are today, you must have the ability to do so or it probably won't help somebody be very successful.

'Definition: not counterfeit or artificial real; True'.

# STRATEGIC
## Strategies for Growing Your Company.

Many corporate strategies have growth- in sales, revenues, profitability, market share, and other dimensions- as the ultimate objective. For that reason, the articles in this section focus on strategies for spurring and maintaining growth. Business writer Theodore Kinni opens the section with his article "How Strategic Is Your Sales Strategy?" which explores the tactics that high- performing companies use to enhance sales by infusing their sales forces with a more vigorous sense of strategy.

Kinni presents several practices for enhancing sales. For example," put the right people in the right seats" that is, hire the right people into your sales organization. CIBA vision developed a profiling instrument that attempts to match the personality traits of prospective account executives with those found in the company's top performing salespeople. The resulting profile then became the basis of a tool the firm uses when hiring. Seeking specific traits in new hires gives CIBA vision the type of people it needs to be successful.

Business writer Adrian Mello stays with the theme of growth in "Creative Destruction or Concentrating on the Core: Witch Is the Right Path to Growth?" As the rate of change has accelerated dramatically, Mello rights, companies must continually reinvent themselves- sometimes even exiting successful business in order to move into more profitable ones. That is, constantly focusing on your core business may not always be sufficient to ensure sustainable growth.

Yet your core business can help you fuel new growth by enabling you to expand into "profitable adjacencies" (businesses that are closely related to your core). While evaluating adjacencies, make sure you have clearly defined core. Then look for the opportunities nearby with the most potent sources of competitive differentiation and advantage- for example, new products, new channels, new customer segments, new geographies, new value chain steps, new technologies, and new businesses that share customer bases of manufacturing processes with core.

This section concludes with "The Latest Thinking on Growth," which distills advice from three books on the subject: Robert Tomasko's Go for Growth! Richard Whiteley and Dianne Hessan's Customer Centered Growth, and Dwight Gertz and Joao P.A. Baptista's Grow to Be Great. By sifting through these books, you can find numerous generic strategies for stimulating growth. One strategy is to grow by selling ever more to the same base of carefully selected customer those- those representing the same base of carefully selected customers- those representing the lion's share of your profits. For example, USAA initially sold auto insurance to military officers and then began providing them with a full portfolio of financial services- to the of $6billion a year. Another growth strategy entails rethinking how you get your product or service to customers. To illustrate, by selling home improvement materials direct to consumer though its stores, The Home Depot became the distribution channel for its industry- and sucked up much of the profit that used to go to manufacturers or less efficient middlemen.

In addition to the need to enhance growth, your unit or company may face other challenges that require savvy strategies. The articles in this section explore three such challenges and provide suggestion for crafting strategies. The articles in this section explore three such challenges and provide suggestions for crafting strategies that will help you overcome each.

In "Taking Advantage of a Downturn," Bain consultants Sarabjit Singh Baveja, Steve Ellis, and Darrell K. Rigby maintain that a recession, though painful, can actually present valuable opportunities for companies. By defining the right strategy, you can seize advantage of an economic downturn- and score impressive profits. For example, "In 2001, Dell computer grew unit sales by 11% even as industry sales declined 12%.Realizing that price elasticity sometimes increases during a recession, Dell used sensible price cuts to gain more than six points in U.S. market share and, in the toughest period of all- the fourth quarter of 2001- to capture more than 90% of the profits in its industry."

How to pursue a thoughtful and balanced recession strategy? Identify your key strengths and weaknesses and use them to measure new strategic options. Also maintain strategic discipline: if the data says your core business is weak, don't try to invest during the downturn until you've fixed the problem. In addition, correct any wrong turns promptly, reevaluating your strategy if it isn't showing results.

In "Strategies for the Shorthand," Paul Michelman turns to a strategic challenge that's far closer to home: maintaining your unit's performance even if the unit finds itself on the wrong end of a workforce reduction. Under these tough circumstances, staying focused is a must. Examine each of your goals, and ask questions such as "Is this goal aligned with the company's strategy?" How will it satisfy stakeholders?" and does my unit have the resources to achieve this goal?" Also, "remember the little picture." Use small successes as a motivational tool, and make sure everyone in your unit understand the long-term strategy. Set weekly and even daily priorities to ensure that short term achievements support longer- term goals.

The final article in this section is "How to Think Strategically About Outsourcing," by business writer Martha Craumer. This selection addresses the challenges posed by companies' increasing interest in outsourcing not only everyday business processes (such as payroll and IT) but strategically significant functions (such as manufacturing and logistics). Yet despite outsourcing's promise, only 54% of companies are satisfied with it, down from more than 80% fifteen years ago.

How to get more from outsourcing? Use it as a tool to drive strategic value transform businesses, and even reshape industry dynamics. For example, Fender Guitar extracted valuable services from UPS supply Chain Solutions (SCS). SCS helped helped Fender rethink its decentralized, country-by-country distribution model in Europe by drawing on best practices from high-tech industry. Now, instead of keeping stacks of inventory in each country, Fender uses a centralized, pan European system that cuts inventory, warehousing and transportation costs.

As you read the selections in this volume, consider how you might start applying the insights and practices offered by the article authors. For example.

How do you and other managers in your organization currently plan strategy? What changes, if any, would help improve the planning process? For example, could you find more effective ways to avoid the cognitive biases that typically figure into strategic planners? Could you create some "simple rules" for distinguishing the most promising strategic opportunities from the merely possible?

. Which of your strategic skills- including alignment, risk management, strategic flexibility- could most benefit from strengthening? And how might you enhance those skills? For instance, could you tighten the alignment between your unit and high-level corporate strategy by gathering more input from employee on how their daily work can help support the company's strategy?

. What strategies is your company currently using to spur growth-whether it's in sales, revenues profit margin, market share, or some other measure? For example, could your company make better use of its core competencies to expand into adjacent businesses?

Is your unit or company currently operating during an economic downturn? Is the organization- understaffed? How might you apply the ideas in this volume to surmounting one or more of these three special challenges?

Harvard Business School Press, Boston Massachusetts/ A Timesaving Guide, RDM, The Results-Driven Manager, Executing Strategy for Business Results pg.12 par.1- pg.17

# STRATEGIC MINDED

We live in a time of accelerating change in the business landscape. Technological advances shift in customer preferences, regulatory changes, globalization, new competitors – these and other complex forces are buffeting organizations like never before. To survive and thrive under these conditions, companies must constantly formulate effective strategies- their plans for differentiating themselves from competitors. And they must execute those strategies flawlessly.

Defining and carrying out a competitive strategy requires tight coordination among managers and employees at every level in your organization. Everyone must not only understand the strategic direction the company is aiming for; they also must ensure that their everyday efforts support that strategy. When top management, you your peers, and employees are all pulling in the same direction, you generate valuable business results:

- You watch your company grow and stay ahead of rivals.
- You identify and seize advantage of profitable new opportunities- for example, serving new markets through innovative products and services, or achieving unprecedented efficiency in your operations.
- You make smarter decisions about how to invest your time, energy, and budgetary dollars by channeling those resources only into initiatives that support your company's strategy.

· You surmount daunting business challenges more deftly – such as helping your organizations succeed during an economic downturn or running your unit or department at top performance even if you're short- staffed.

As appealing as these advantages are, planning and executing strategy isn't easy. Indeed, many strategic initiatives never get off the ground. Why? During the planning stage alone, you face numerous difficult decisions- and you risk making a serious misstep at each one. For example, you have to figure out which of the many new developments you see happening in the business have important ramifications for your company. Does a change in consumer taste, for instance, constitute a threat to your current offerings – or an opportunity to serve an entirely new market profitably? How will you avoid the all- too common cognitive biases that can lead to inadvisable strategies- such as assuming that customers will want the new product you're designing or that a strategy which worked in the past will work just as well now?

Also, how far out should you look as you craft a competitive strategy- three years? Five? Fifteen? And of the many possible strategic scenarios you believe could emerge on the business horizon, how do you determine which of them is most likely to take shape- and when? Moreover, at any point in time, the changes unfolding in the business arena represent a wide variety of alluring opportunities. How should you decide which of them to pursue? Of the changes that pose threats, how will you determine which of them is the most serious?

Clearly, strategic planning is rife with questions and potential pitfalls. But even if you resolve those questions and sidestep the pitfalls, your well-informed and brilliantly crafted strategy will prove useless unless you can execute it skillfully. To put your strategy into action, you must master a broad range of skills.

For example, you need to align your unit behind the corporate strategy. Alignment means identifying the specific unit- level actions, performance, and projects that will best support the high-level strategy that your company has defined. If you lead the marketing team for example, which marketing strategies will most help your company achieve its strategic goal of carving out new markets or winning a reputation as a cost leader in its industry? If you head a customer call center, how might you redesign key processes to support your organization's objective of increasing customer loyalty and profitability?

Even after you've achieved this alignment, you'll need to maintain it when circumstances shift yet again. For example, what will you do if you lose several crucial, talented employees to rival firms? When the technology you're using becomes obsolete? When an unforeseen competitor suddenly looms on the horizon and changes all the rules of the game? Maintaining alignment in the face of continual change requires strategic flexibility- another essential skill.

Thankfully, mastering the skills needed to define and carry out strategy is possible. And this volume will help you. You'll find one section devoted entirely to tactics for planning your strategy. Other concentrates on strengthening your strategic skills- including creating and maintaining strategic alignment, managing the risks involved in selecting and following a strategic direction, and remaining flexible in your strategies. An additional section focuses on strategies for growing your company, since profitable growth plays a central role in in any organization's health and competitive positioning. The final section explores a set of special strategic challenges you might expect to encounter- surviving an economic downturn, running your department when you're understaffed, getting competitive advantage from outsourcing- and lays out suggestions for tackling those challenges.

Here's a closer look at what you'll find in this volume:

### Planning Your Strategy.

Many managers find strategic planning challenging. The articles in the section introduce common planning pitfalls and provide guidelines for circumventing them. In "Strategic Planning- Why It's Not Just for Senior Managers Anymore," business writer Marie Gendron starts things off by making a compelling business case for what she calls "expanded strategic planning involve a broad range of managers and employees in development of strategy-and get remarkable results.

For example, Electronic Data Systems gathered input from a major cross section of employees on where the company stood in its markets, what its current strengths and weaknesses were, and where its future opportunities lay. It then used that input to map out a three-year strategic plan. The approach paid big dividends- in the form of significant market expansion and jump in revenues. Gordon provides tips for designing an expanded strategic planning process- including ensuring that everyone knows how the company is doing financially and arming all workers with the strategic information they need to do their jobs in a way that furthers the company's market goals.

In "Cognitive Bias in Everyday Strategic Planning business writer Loren Gary introduces several common mental barriers that can figure into managers during the strategic planning process and explains how to avoid them. For example, one cognitive bias causes managers to seek only information confirming their assumption that a particular product or service will appeal to consumers. To counteract this bias, you need to systematically take the opposite perspective- putting yourself in customers' shoes and asking, "why might this product fail?"

Another bias causes manager to assume that a strategic alliance that worked for one project (such as a co- marketing agreement with another company) should be repeated for other projects. To combat this bias, broaden your information base by involving in the decision- making session more people than would typically participate. Change participants to present disconfirming evidence for why repeating a strategic alliance may not be wise for a new project- no matter how successful it was on a previous effort.

The next article, "Scenario Planning Reconsidered," introduces scenario planning as a strategy formulation tool and explains how to get the most from it. Through scenario planning, managers use their intuition and imagination to craft stories about how their industry might evolve in the future. They then design a strategy for responding to each scenario, should it actually arise. How to use scenario planning? Start by asking people for their views about future developments. Then gather and analyze data on the various trends that effect your business. Sketch out scenarios- "what if" stories depicting how your industry's most influential forces might play out. Assess the implications of each scenario has begun to materialize. Finally, reassess your vision in light of the scenarios, asking yourself whether the vision requires any changes.

The last article in this section is "How to Evaluate Opportunities Quickly and Strategically," by business editor Kirsten D Sandberg. As Sandberg points out, changes in the business world can create such a large sea of possibilities that can capsize a company while it's trying to decide which ones to pursue. To avoid this out- come, establish "simple rules" for identifying the few opportunities you want to explore among the many possibilities out there.

For instance, "boundary rules" enable you to distinguish opportunities that align with your company's core ideology from those that don't. American Express, for example, forges strategic partnerships with only those firms that can deliver unique benefits- not simply "me too" results- to Amex's customers. Amex also insists on priority access to the partner's resources and information. Moreover, partners must have the infrastructure needed to meet Amex's service requirements. "Exit rules are also useful: they help you determine when to "cut bait." To illustrate, Amex establishers performance objectives for each of its strategic partners and ties its exit strategy to those objectives.

## Strengthening Your Strategic Skills.

To implement a well-planned strategy, you need a set of strategic skills. The articles in this section lay out those skills and offer suggestions for strengthening them. Business editor Paul Michelman begins the section by introducing the first of three articles on strategic alignment. In "How Will You Better Align with Strategy?" he defines the three steps necessary to align your unit behind your company's strategy: (1) Make sure you have a clear understanding of the strategy, (2) Turn that strategy into something actionable for your staff, and (3) Implement procedures that will keep your unit aligned with the strategy despite shifting conditions.

Michelman then provides recommendation for handling step 1 if your company hasn't explicitly defined the high- level strategy. For example, "Begin by asking. Seek your boss's interpretation and, where appropriate, reach even higher. Look not only for face-to-face input, speeches by the CEO, reports to shareholders, and other documents can reveal valuable insights." Then "compare what you hear and read about strategic priorities with where the company's resources are going. There may be a lot of talk about innovation, but if the biggest portions of the expenditure pie are earmarked for marketing the existing product line, that says something quite different."

In "How Will You Turn Top- Level Strategy into unit Level Action?" Michelman turns to step 2 of the strategic alignment processes. To convert corporate strategy into an actionable agenda for your unit, communicate the strategy to your employees using relevant context and language. Involve your team in defining how the strategy relates to your unit and what alignment will require. Then ensure that each direct report is on board- and on track. By directly involving your employees in discussion on how to execute strategy in your unit, you can greatly enhance their commitment to the strategy and to their individual roles in carrying out.

Michelman's "How Will You Maintain Alignment?" Explores step 3 of the alignment process by providing suggestions for keeping. "everyone's eyes on the strategic prize" despite shifting circumstances. One idea is to "connect each project to strategy" by ensuring that projects are completed on time and within budget and that they advance the company as far as possible toward its strategic objectives. Also, "measure and reward" strategic performance by custom building metric and reward systems to support the strategy. For example, tie a portion of your team's total compensation to its results as they relate to top-line strategy.

Finally, "wage war on short-term thinking." Help employees shift their attention from scoring short-term gains (such as exceeding this month's revenue targets) to ensuring long-term focus on the strategy. You can encourage long -term focus by giving each employee a document with the annual corporate objectives listed on the top- and asking each to write down five to six initiatives he or she needs to accomplish during the year to help the company meet its goals.

In addition to alignment, strategic skills include managing the risk involved in setting and implementing strategy. Loren Gary's article "The Right Kind of Failure" addresses this issue of risk. Whether your strategy involves innovating radical new products or services, defining new markets, or overhauling your business model, it will have in inherent risks. For example, perhaps an initiative designed to support the strategy will fail, experience delays, or cost much more than you expected. Or maybe competitive forces will take a turn you didn't anticipate- rendering your new strategy useless.

Though risk is inherent in any strategy, avoidance of risk at all costs won't help your company. To enable managers and employees to design and carry out strategy despite the risk, you need to create a safe environment for experimenting and for learning from mistakes. Guidelines include initiating experiments (such as prototypes for new products) with the assumptions about what you might learn, assessing initiatives' outcomes as quickly as possible, experimenting on a small scale, so that any failure will have relatively minor ramifications.

In "Five Steps to Thriving in Times of Uncertainty," business writer Peter Jacobs focuses on flexibility, another important strategic skill. To maintain strategic flexibility- ability to confront change and uncertainty by adjusting your strategy- Jacobs offers several suggestions. For example, view strategic decisions as a portfolio of options. "Organizations usually have multiple projects and initiatives underway simultaneously," he writes, "and it's critical that leaders not let one or two dominate their attention. As markets shift, seemingly less significant initiatives may become the most valuable." Also continually gather fresh perspectives on the strategic situation, for instance, by routinely rotating managers through different roles so they can get the "big picture" of how your company operates. And partner with other firms to mutually capitalize on complementary resources and gain fresh ideas and insights on what's happening in your industry.

Management consultant John Hagel III provides additional thoughts about strategic flexibility in his article. "Web Service: Technology as a catalyst for Strategic Thinking." According to Hagel, Web services-technologies that automate connections across applications and data- can enhance flexibility and collaboration within an organization. With greater flexibility and collaboration, you reduce inefficiency and mobilize more resources to deliver great value to customers. For example, Dell computer uses Web services to connect with suppliers and third-party logistics providers in ways that enable Dell to assemble computer to order with unusual speed- a competency essential to its strategy and business model.

Harvard Business School Press, Boston Massachusetts/A Timesaving Guide, RDM, The Results-Driven Manager, Executing Strategy for Business Results pg. 1 – pg.12

# SIMPLIFYING

Due to such abundant work orders and heavy overloads incredible lines and enormous wait times, you can help by simplifying and making thing a lot easier by doing so it saves a lot of time and money to strategically just simplify the work order or to make or reduce for lessor the workload and it will benefit you. And because of it you will get more done, and takes less money to do the work, and whole lot of less time, and whole lot less money usually means it's profitable and more beneficial for you as the worker. At the office or on the job or whatever it is, that you are doing at this time.

'Definition: to make simpler or less complex – simplification n.'.

# PINPOINTING

Strategically Pinpointing your opponent next board move or strategical strategy alignment reviewing and responding and reacting to this person next move in a contest of informal or not so formal reaction. Being aware of the consequences and what might occur or happen from these actions being Strategic Minded and to respond and to react for your yourself they say a best defense is your best offence. That's what going to win a lot of games. And that you will win a lot people over, and that will give you the respect you should have, and you will have a lot of success in life with the people you meet and will develop a heroin over you and people will have a lot of respect for you! and have a lot of confidence in you! and the things you do! And in the strategy's that you use, so mostly respected, mostly confident and well know as a champion or top contender in your field.

'Definition: To locate precisely- ad. Precise'.

# RESOURCEFUL

Essential for Organizations and Marketing are all apart of human resources and are resourceful for a higher level of Management. "The four levels of disciplines" cover the essential planner for team building and Human resources always be helpful and courteous too.

Team building which requires a trust level and accountability that builds team planning in which is designed for the office or at home with friends and family. Such as touching and values play a part of the planning such goals as something you might enjoy on doing these are goals, we use guidelines and there are certain criteria's that need to be met when setting these goals. This includes the hiring of a new employee or employee's, what the importance's are, and what the criteria of the company are,  or certain criteria of the new employer are, through the interview to find out what the demands are and find out if it's essential to the wants and needs of the Company, or Organization, or even what the employee wants to be a part of as a team, and as a new employee.

'Definition: adj. able to deal effectively with problems.

The Four Obsessions of an Extraordinary Executive, 123 help me .com 14 Feb. 2015

# SYNERGIZE
## Principles of Creative Cooperation

Synergy is the essence of principle- centered leadership. It is the essence of principle-centered parenting. It catalyzes, unifies, and unleashes the greatest powers within people. All the habits we have covered prepare us to create the miracle of synergy.

What is synergy? Simply defined, it means that the whole is greater than than the sum of its parts. It means that the relationship which the parts have to each other is a part in and of itself. It is not only a part, but the most catalytic, the most empowering, the most unifying, and the most exciting part

The creative process is also the most terrifying part because you don't know exactly what's going to happen or where it is going to lead. You don't know what new dangers and challenges you'll find. It takes an enormous amount of internal security to begin with the spirit of adventure, the spirit of discovery, the spirit of creativity. Without doubt, you have to leave the comfort zone of base camp and confront an entirely new and unknown wilderness. You become a trailblazer, a pathfinder. You open new possibilities, new territories, new continents, so that other can follow.

Synergy is everywhere in nature. If nature. If you plant two plants close together, the roots comingle and improve the quality of the soil so that both plants will grow better than if there separated. If you put two pieces of wood together, they will hold much they will hold for much more than the weight held by each separately. The whole is greater than the sum of its parts. One plus one equals three or more.

The challenge is to apply the principles of creative cooperation, which we learn from nature, in our interactions. Family life provides many opportunities to observe synergy and to practice it. the very way that a man and a woman bring a child into the world is 'synergistic'. The essence of synergy is to value differences- to respect them, to build on strengths, to compensate for weaknesses.

We obviously value the physical differences between men and women, husband and wives. But what about the social, mental and emotional differences? Could these differences not also be sources of creating new, exciting forms of life- creating an environment that is truly fulfilling for each person, that nurtures the self-esteem and self-worth of each, that creates opportunities for each to mature into independence and then gradually into interdependence? Could synergy not create a new script for the next generation- one that is more geared to service and contribution, and is less protective, less adversarial, less self; one that is more open, more trusting, more giving, and less defensive, protective, and political; one that is more loving, more caring, and less possessive and judgmental?

The 7 HABITS OF HIGHLY EFFECTIVE PEOPLE, Restoring the Character Ethic, STEPHEN R. COVEY, Simon and Schuster, pg.262 par.3 - pg.263

# NEGATIVE SYNERGY

Seeking the third alternative is a major paradigm shift from the dichotomous, either/or mentality, but look at the differences in results!

How much negative energy is typically expended when people try to solve problems or make decisions in an interdependent reality? How much time is spent in confessing other people's sins, politicking, rivalry, interpersonal conflict, protecting one's back-side, masterminding, and second guessing? It's like trying to drive down the road with one foot on the gas and the other foot on the brake.

And instead of getting a foot off the brake, most people give it more gas. They try to apply more pressure, more eloquence, more logical information to strengthen their position.

The problem is that highly dependent people are trying to succeed in an interdependent reality. They're either dependent on borrowing strength from position power and they go for Lose/Win. They may talk Win/Win technique, but they don't really want to listen; they want to manipulate. And synergy can't thrive in that environment.

Insecure people think that all reality should be amenable to their paradigms. They have a high need to clone others, to mold them over to their own thinking. They don't realize that the very strengths of the relationship is in having another point of view. Sameness is not oneness; uniformity is not unity. Unity, or oneness,

Is complementariness, not sameness. Sameness is uncreative… and boring. The essence of synergy is to value the differences I've come to believe that the key to interpersonal synergy is intrapersonal synergy, that is synergy within ourselves. The heart of intrapersonal synergy is embodied in the principles in the first three Habits, which give the internal security sufficient to handle the risks of being open and vulnerable. By internalizing those principles, we develop the abundance mentality of Win/Win and the authenticity of Habit 5

One of the very practical results of being the principle- centered is that it makes us whole- truly integrated. People who are scripted deeply in logical, verbal, left-brain thinking will discover how totally inadequate that thinking is in solving problems which require a great deal of creativity. They become aware and begin to open up a new script inside their right brain. It's not that the right brain wasn't there; it just lay dormant. The muscles had not been developed, or perhaps they had atrophied after early childhood because of the heavy left-brain emphasis of formal education or social scripting.

When a person has access to both the intuitive, creative, and visual right brain, and the analytical, logical, verbal left-brain, then the whole brain is working. In others words, there is psychic synergy taking place in our own head. And this tool is best suited to the reality of what life is, because life is not just logical- it is also emotional.

One day I was presenting a seminar which I titled, "Manage from the left, lead from the Right" to a company in Orlando. Florida. During the break, the president of the company came up to me and said, "Stephen, this is intriguing. But I have been thinking about this material more in terms of it's application to my marriage than to my Business. My wife and I have real communication problem. I wonder if you would have lunch with me two of us and just kind of watch how we talk to each other?"

"Let's do It," I replied

As we sat down together, we exchanged a few pleasantries. Then this man turned to his wife and said, Now, honey I've invited Stephen to have lunch with us to see if he could help us in our communication with each other. I know you feel I should be a more sensitive, considerate husband. Could you give me something specific you think I ought to do?" His dominant right brain wanted facts, figures, specifics, parts.

"Well, as I've told you before, it's nothing specific. It's more of a general sense I have about priorities." Her dominant right brain was dealing with sensing and with the gestalt, the whole, the relationship between the parts.

THE 7 HABITS OF HIGHLY EFFECTIVE PEOPLE, Restoring the Character Ethic, STEPHEN R. COVEY, Simon and Schuster, pg.274 par.4 - pg.275 par.7

# EMPATHY

Whenever you feel overloaded, anxious, or fearful, take some quite time to lower your stimulation level. Being alone to recharge will help you decompress. Remember to turn of the computer and phone. Sit in a comfortable position and take a few deep breaths to relax your body. Feel the stillness and ease as tension begins to melt away. There is nothing to do and nothing to be. Just breathe and relax. When thoughts come, let them drift by like clouds in the sky. Do not attach to them. Focus only on slowly inhaling and then exhaling. Feel stress leaving your body as you connect to a sense of serenity.

In this tranquil inner space. Visualize a large tree with a wide. Strong trunk that extends down the center of your body. From head to toe. Take a few moments to feel its power and vibrant energy. Then visualize the tree's roots growing from the bottom of your feet and rooting down into the ground. Make their way deeper and deeper creating an uncomfortable sense of solidity. Focus on these roots when you are anxious or afraid. Let the roots anchor you into Mother Earth stabilizing you. Rooting yourself in this way provides an inner strength that will keep you centered and protected when life gets overwhelming. As you gently and slowly open your eyes, continue to feel the sensation of grounding. Comeback to the outer world knowing that you can use this visualization to anchor yourself whenever you get thrown off balance. Grounding is essential skill to keep you strong. Focusing on your feet, not your fears or sense of overwhelm, is a quick way to center yourself. Foot massage also works wonders to get you out of your head and into your body. Regularly practice this Earthing meditation, as well as others I'll be sharing, to reduce sensory overload.

**Blessing of Being an Empath.**

As you begin this journey with me, remember that your presence, your sweetness, your tender appreciation for people and all of life are gifts, for you and others. Your intuition and your refined sensitivities are healing. I want you to appreciate yourself, your openness and your ability to feel. Realize how special and how perfect you are. When you really see yourself, you can connect with the wholeness and depth within. Then you can enjoy your empathy- and that's the point. Not everyone will understand you, but that's okay. Search for kindred spirits who will, and you will understand them too. It's a beautiful feeling of connection. Later, I will discuss how to create empath support groups by using this book and its companion audio program, essential tools for empath, In the support group. In the support groups, you can read sections of the book or listen to the audio and then discuss how the information relates to your issues as empaths, it's amazingly freeing to give and receive such support.

We are in the midst of an evolution of human consciousness, and empath are the path forgers. A sacred responsibility comes with our sensitivities, witch demand more of us than simply retreating into isolation. It's vital we learn how to avoid feeling overwhelmed so we can fully shin our power in the world. Empath and all sensitive people are pioneers on the forefront of a new way of being for humankind.

You are part of Generation S, for Sensitivity- those who salute compassion and loving and kindness. You represent a vital opening for humanity to grow into a more heart- centered and intuitive awareness. You can model for others how to be sensitivities and powerful.

I am passionate about helping you manage your sensitivities and use them for your personal well- being and the greater good. Just as I've learned to honor myself as an empath, which makes me feel incredibly whole, I hope you will honor your gifts too. I want the information in this book to empower you to be more yourself than you ever have been. To begin this journey, I offer you the following Empath Affirmation. (I Vow to honor my sensitivities and treat myself lovingly as I explore what it means to be an Empath and embrace my gifts, I will appreciate myself every day.)

Judith Orloff, MD. The Empath's Survival Guide/Life Strategies for Sensitive People pg.25 - pg.27

# FINDING THE RIGHT WORK

Some jobs are more satisfying and less stressful for empaths than others, for us to excel or enjoy our work, we want to make the most of our sensitivities, intuition, thoughtfulness, quietness, and creativity- and we don't want to try to be someone we're not.

**The Best for Empaths.**

I am often asked which careers and working conditions are ideal for empaths. Traditionally, they do better in low- stress jobs with smaller companies or on their own. Empaths are usually happier working at home, away from the office frenzy. Emotional vampires are much easier to deal with by email, phone, you can plan your schedule and regular breaks to decompress.

Many of empath patients prefer being self- employed because they avoid the drain of overwhelm coworkers, bosses, and packed schedules. Empaths tend to do better managing their own time rather than having to attend the frequent team meetings that large businesses require (unless the team is positive and cohesive). One empath told me, "I started a home business after many failed attempts at trying to function in offices. I feel much more energized and happier being my own boss." Another empath shared with me, "I'm a seamstress working from home. I could never be in an office forty hours a week. The smells, sound, and lights make me ill,"

If you're employed by a business, it may be feasible to arrange a part-time home office situation and do your work virtually, with ongoing access to the Internet, emails, texts, and Skype. Increasingly, people don't always have to be tied to their office to do their job well, a perk for empaths that allows them to have more choice in their work location. One empath who set up a location- independent business offers this advice to sensitive people: "I used to work for a corporation and was drained by office politics/ Now I work by Skype, and it's fantastic. Think about what you love to do and where your skill set is. Then see if you can find a way to share this via the internet. It's the way the new workplace is going."

However, whether you work at home or alone in an office, be careful not to become isolated or to push yourself too hard. Balance your alone time with people time among colleagues and friends. Some of my empath patients have found that working part-time from home is ideal. You can break up the isolation by scheduling outside meetings. An empath financial advisor who does this said,' "I like working Independently and meeting one on one with clients in different places. I'm not stuck in an office or at home, and I can arrange my own schedule." All these options may be preferable to the sensory overload of driving to work in heavy traffic or staying in an office eight or more hours a day. Time management is key.

How do these considerations translate into real-world jobs? Empaths do well be self-employed business owners, writers, editors, artists, and in other creative professions. Many actors and musicians, such as Claire Danes, Alanis Morrissette, Scarlett Johansson, and Jim Carey, have admitted that they are "highly sensitive."

Other god jobs include Website AND Graphic designers, virtual assistants, accountants or lawyers with home offices, and independent electricians and contractors a d plumber who can set their own appointments. Being a real- estate agent or roving business consultant can be fine too, as long as you establish good boundaries about when you can be reached, and you don't over schedule yourself. Landscape design and gardening, forestry, or other employment that puts you in nature is wonderful for empaths, as are jobs preserving the earth and the ecosystem.

Many empaths also go into helping professions because of their big hearts and desires to serve others. They become physicians, nurses, dentists, physical therapists, psychotherapists, social workers, teachers, Yoga instructors, Chinese medical practitioners, massage therapists, clergy, hospice workers, life coaches, and employees or volunteers for non- profit organizations, among other heartfelt jobs. Working with animals, animal rescue, and veterinary medicine are gratifying choices too. But to thrive, empaths in the helping professions must learn how not to take on the symptoms and stress of their patients and clients, a skill I'll discuss later in this chapter. Occupations such as a police officer or firefighter, though heroic, may be too stressful for an empath because of the high sensory stimulation and ongoing physical and emotional trauma inherent in these roles.

Empaths can excel when they use their intuition and compassion to contribute to well- being of others. One empath patient told me, "I'm a good college professor because I can feel when a student needs extra help." Another empath said, "I am effective administrator because people are comfortable coming to me. They know I will understand them." Although empaths receive great satisfaction from helping others, we tend to over give, which puts us at risk for burnout. Even so. When empath in the helping professions practice self- care strategies, they can have gratifying careers that improve the lives of many.

Empath are valuable in a host of careers. However, you need to find the right work that supports your skills, gifts and temperament. An Empath's attributes may not be as appreciated in places such as corporations, academia, professional sports, the military, or government. A better match may be the helping professions, the arts, and the organizations with more humanistic awareness. So, use your intuition to sense if you are good fit with the mission and shared goals of an enterprise, it's people, and the space and energy of the environment. Just because a job looks good on paper doesn't mean it's right for you. It has to feel right in your gut and your body too.

Judith Orloff, MD the Empath's Survival Guide/ Life Strategies for Sensitive People pg.170 par.1 - pg. 173

# LEADER

Teams also vary in terms, traditional manager Teams- led the teams in management in which the manager services as a Team Leader. The manager assigns work to the other team members. These types of teams are the most natural to form, with managers having the power to hire and fire team members and being held for the team's results.

Self-managed teams that manage themselves and do not report directly to a supervisor. Instead, team members select their own leader. And they may even take turns in the Leadership role. They're a new form of team that rose in popularity with the Total Quality Movement in the 1980's. Unlike manager-led teams. These teams manage themselves and do not report directly to a supervisor. Instead team members select their own leader, and they may take turns in the leadership role, Self-managed teams also have the power to select new team members. As a whole, the team shares responsibility for a significant task, such as assembly of an entire car. The task is ongoing rather than a temporary task such as a charity fund drive for a given year.

Organization begin to use self- managed teams as away to reduce hierarchy by allowing team members to complete task and solve problems on their own. The benefits of self- managed teams extend much further. Research has shown that employee in self-managed teams have higher job satisfaction, increased self-esteem and grow more on the job. The benefits to the Organization include increased productivity, Increased flexibility, and lower turnover. Self -managed teams can be found at all levels of the organizations, and they bring particular benefits to lower level employees by giving them a sense of ownership of their jobs that that they may not otherwise have. The increased satisfaction can also reduce absenteeism, because employees don't want to let their team member down.

Typical team goals are improving quality, reducing costs, and meeting deadlines. Teams also have a "stretch" goal- a goal that is difficult reach but important to the business unit. Many teams also have special project goals. Texas Instruments (TI), a company that makes semi-conductors, used self-direct teams to make improvements in work process. Teams were allowed to set their own goals in conjunction with other managers and other teams. TI added an individual component to the typical team compensation system. The individual component reward team members for learning new skills that added to their knowledge. These "knowledge blocks" Include topics such as leadership, administration, and problem solving. The team decides what additional skills people might need to help the team meet its objectives. Team members would then take classes and/ or otherwise demonstrate their proficiency in the new skill on the job in order to get certification for mastery of the skill. Individuals could then be evaluated based on their contribution to the team and how they are building skills to support the team.

Self- managed teams are empowered teams, Teams that have the responsibility as well as the authority to achieve their goals, which means they have the responsibility as well as the authority to achieve their goals. Team members have the power to control tasks and processes and to make decisions. Research shows that self- managed might be a higher risk of suffering from negative outcomes due to conflict, so its important that they are supported with training to help them deal with conflict effectively. Self- managed teams may sill have a leader who helps them coordinate with the larger organization. For a product team composed of engineering, production and marketing employees, being empowered means that the team can decide everything about a products appearance, production and costs without having to get permission or sign off from a higher management. As a result of empowered teams can more effectively meet tighter deadlines at AT&T Inc., for example, the model -4200 phone team cut development time in half while lowering costs and improving quality by using the empowered team approach. A special form of self-managed team approach. A special form of self- managed teams is self-directed teams A special form of self- managed teams where members are determined who will lead them with external oversight, which also determine who will lead them with no external oversight.

http//catalog. flatworldsknowledge.com/bookhub/reader 9/13

# RESILIENT AND BRILLIANT
## Defining the Characteristics of Desirable Candidates.

Employers look for many qualities in candidates. The following list gives you an idea of the qualities consider most important when hiring new employees. Other characteristics may be particularly important to you, your company, and the job your looking fill. This list gives you a good start in identifying them:

(Hardworking:) Hard work can often overcome lack of experience or training. You want to hire people who are willing to do whatever it takes to get the job done. Conversely, no amount of skill can make up for a lack of initiative or work ethic. Although you won't know for sure until you make your hire, carefully questioning candidates can give you some idea of their work ethic. (or, at least, what they want you to believe about their work ethic). Of course, hard work alone isn't always the end-all, be-all of hiring. People can generate a lot of work, but if the work doesn't align with your business's strategies or isn't with in the true scope of their role, then it's wasted effort. Be carful to note the difference as you assess your candidates.

(Good attitude:) Although what constitutes a "good "attitude differs for each person, positive, friendly, willing-to-help perspective makes life at the office much more enjoyable and makes everyone's job easier. When you interview candidates, consider what they'll be like to work with for the next five or ten years. Skills are important, but attitude is even more important. This is the mantra for success of SouthWest Airlines: "Hire for attitude, train for skill."

(Experienced:) Some candidates may naively think they should be hired immediately based on weight of their institution's diploma. However, they may lack a critical element that is so important in the hiring process: experience. An interview gives you the opportunity to ask pointed questions that require your candidates to demonstrate that they can do the job.

(Self-Starter:) Candidates needs to demonstrate an ability to take initiative to get work done. Initiative ranks as a top reason employee are able to get ahead where they work.

(Team Player:) Teamwork is critical to the success of today's organization that must do far more with far fewer resources than their predecessors. The ability to work with others and collaborate effectively is definite must for employees today.

(Smart:) Smart people can often find better and quicker solution to the problems that confront them. In the world of business, work smarts are more important than book smarts (present book excepted, of course)

(Responsible:) You want to hire people who are willing to take on the responsibilities of their positions. Questions about the kinds of projects your candidates have been responsible for an exact role those projects played in their success can help you determine this important quality. Finer points, like showing up for the interview and remembering the name of the company they're interviewing for, can also be key indicators of your candidates' sense of responsibility.

(Flexible/Resilient:) Employees who are able to multitask and switch directions if necessary, in a seamless manner are real assets to any organization in today's fast-changing world.

(Cultural fit:) Every business has its own unique culture and set of values. The ability to fit into culture and values is key to whether candidates can succeed within a particular business (assuming that they already have the technical skills).

(Stable:) You don't want to hire someone today and then find out he's already looking for the next position tomorrow. No business can afford the expense of hiring and training a new employee, only to have that person leave six months later. You can get some indication of a person's potential stability (or lacked thereof) by asking pointed questions about how long candidates worked with a previous employer and why they left. Be especially thorough and methodical as you probe this particular area.

Starting a Business All- In-One for dummies, 2nd Edition, A Wiley Brand 6 Books in one! / Eric Tyson, MBA, Bob Nelson, Ph.D., et al.pg.388 par.4 – pg.390

# REALISM

Notice that the same sentences are true under both of his reference-assignments, the sentences we accept generate the same experiential expectations under both schemes, the behavior that is associated with believing- true or desiring- true particular sentences in the same under both schemes, and if the expectations we have or the things we do are successful (respectively, unsuccessful) the sentence we are then required to accept by our operational and theoretical criteria are the same and their truth values are the same.

Its amused God for a while to see men and women talking to each other, never noticing that they were almost never referring to the same objects, properties and relations, but then once again, inevitably, He became bored, so He invented philosophers. (Here caution compels me to the end of parable.)

There are a number of stocks 'easy answers' to the problems of the determination of reference (most of them are discussed in 'Why there isn't a ready-made world'). Thus, a philosopher might say, ' When the child comes to "associate" the world table with certain perceptions, images, etc., he is "associating" it not in the semantical sense (table doesn't refer to the visual impressions which trigger the utterance there is a table in front of me, or whatever), but in a causal sense. He is caused to have certain beliefs, partly by the fact that certain visual impressions occur. But those visual impressions, "mental representation", or whatever, are in turn caused by certain external events. Normally, they are caused by the presence of a table, in fact. So indirectly, the word table comes to be associated with external tables."

To see why this answer isn't a solution to the problem, imagine it being said first by a women philosopher and then by a man philosopher. When the woman says this ( Now we are inside the parable again), she is pointing out that the child's belief there is a table in front of me is a certain relation- the relation effect- to certain visual impressions, and that these are in relation of effect to certain external events. In fact they are caused by presence of a table. When the man says this, he is pointing out that the same visual impressions are caused by the presence of a table, So the word table has come to be associated with tables. Of course they are both right. The word table is 'Indirectly associated' with tables (in the way pointed out by the women). It doesn't follow that there tables (in the way pointed out by the man). It doesn't follow that there in such a thing as the correspondence (the One, metaphysically singled out correspondence) between words and things.

At this point in the dialogue, there is an argument that invariably get from causal realists. This runs somewhat like this: You are caricaturing our position. Ac realist does not claim that reference is fixed by the conceptual connection (i.e., the connection in our theory) between the terms "reference", "causation", "sense impression", etc.; the realist claims that reference is fixed by causation itself.'

Here the philosopher is ignoring his own epistemological position. He is philosophizing as if naïve realism were true of him (or, equivalently, as if he and he alone were in absolute relation to the world). What he calls 'causation' really is causation, and of course there is a fixed, somehow singled-out, correspondence between the word and one definite relation in his case. Or so he assumes. But how this can be so was just the question at issue. (If this isn't clear, just imagine the words said first by a women and then by a man, as before).

A more sophisticated form of the same argument is this: why Your argument only shows that reference is not fixed by anything psychological, anything "inside the head". But that is no problem: why can't reference be fixed by something non-psychological?'

The answer, quite simply, is that the idea that the 'non-psychological' fixes reference- i.e., that nature itself determines what our words stand for- is totally unintelligible. At bottom, to think that a sign- relation is built is built into nature is to revert to medieval essentialism, to the idea that there are 'self- identifying objects ' and ' species out there ( This is discussed at length in 'why there isn't and existence substantial from, etc.) to back it up, but also an elaborate correspondence between two (God had arranged it so that the 'intellectual species' produced by the productive imagination acting on the phantasms would have a context of a twentieth-century world view, by contrast, to say in one's most intimidating tone of voice 'I believe that casual connections determine what our words correspond to' is only to say that one believes in a one-knows- not-what which solves our problem one- knows- not- how.

# ONTOLOGICAL RELATIVITY?

A solution that has occurred to some philosophers is to keep the idea of 'correspondence that is 'fixed', one intended reference- relations. If we take this line, then the word 'table' refers to one definite set of things in an ordinary 'empirical' sense, but not in 'transcendental' sense (not from the standpoint of the metalanguage. When we say that there is one set which is the set of tables and a different set which is the set of tables and a different set which is the set of chairs, that statement is true (construed as an ordinary first-order statement). There is the just one set which is the set of chairs and just one set which is the set of tables in each model, and the set and the set of tables in a model is a different set from the set of chairs in the same model. But that does not mean that there is one set which is the set of chairs in every admissible model. The set of chairs in one model. How we imagine tables and chairs, what experiences we have when we see and touch tables and chairs, what we do in there presence, etc., are all unaffected by the lack of a unique assignment of objects and to our words; the words 'see', 'touch', touch', 'sit down', etc., simply change their change their reference from model in such a way that nothing we can notice is ever affected.

The doctrine just described has been called 'ontological relativity'. It was suggested by Quine (generally he suggests this is the stance to take to all languages other than one's own. Although there are places where he speaks of the reference of even his own terms as 'free floating'.) The doctrine that Davidson calls 'the empty reference theory' is, perhaps, the same doctrine.

This doctrine cannot, however, be accepted. I cannot accept it for my own language, because to do so would turn the notion of an object into a totally metaphysical notion. I know what tables are and what cats and what black holes are. But what am I to make of the notion of an X which is a table or a cat or a black hole (or the number three or...)? An object which has no properties at all in itself and any property you like 'in a model' is an inconceivable Ding a sich. The doctrine of ontological relativity avoids the avoids the problems of medieval philosophy (the problems of classical realism). but it takes on the problems of Kantian metaphysics in their place. Nor can the doctrine be accepted for languages other than my own; the human situation is symmetrical. If other people's words do not determinately refer, then neither do my own. (Quine view is discussed in 'Why reason can't be naturalized'.)

# DISQUOTATIONAL THEORIES OF TRUTH AND REFERENCE.

If the picture of the language user that we have thus far discussed- the picture of (there being) one particular correspondence between what is 'inside' the mind or brain (include language) and what is 'outside'- leads to the metaphysical fantasy of a 'ready-made world', with self -identifying objects, 'built-in' structure, essences or whatever, and the modified picture of the mind or whatever, and the modified picture of the mind or brain simply accepting a whole lot of different correspondence between word and object, leads, to the metaphysical fantasy of a 'noumenal' world, with no determinate relation to our experiential world, then the trouble with this entire discussion must lie at a deeper level. It must lie, in fact, in the common assumptions of both picture: that we understand such notions as 'refers to' and corresponds to' by associating these notations with platonic objects ('correspondence') – assumption has been (usually uncritically and inexplicitly) then the entire systems of competing philosophical theories and arguments unwinds itself with a sort of inevitability. But can we avoid this common assumption?

On this theory, we understand the word 'true' not by associating that word with a property, or a correspondence, but by learning such facts of the obvious.

Realism and Reason , Philosophical Papers, Volume 3 / HILARY PUTNAM, Walter Beverly Pearson Professor of Mathematical Logic, Harvard University, Press Syndicate of the University Cambridge The Pitt Building, Trumpington Street, Cambridge cb2 IRP 32 East 57th Street, New York, NY 10022, USA 296 Beaconsfield Parade, Middle Park, Melbourne 3206, Australia pg. x par. 3 – pg. xiv

# THE VIEW OF MICHAEL DUMMETT

If neither a correspondence theory nor a pure diquotational theory of truth is of much help, the situation reminiscent of a common predicament in philosophy. As Strawson remarked many years ago, we are constantly being asked to choose between metaphysical positions on the one hand and reductionist positions on the other, and what is terribly difficult (but makes the game of philosophy worth the candle) is to show that the metaphysical mystery is not the only alternative to the simplistic position of the reductionist (and, of course, vice versa).

During the years that I was wrestling with the problems I have just described, the first clear indication that a coherent alternative to both the correspondence theory and the pure diquotational theory might be available came from writings of Michael Dummett. Dummett considers the learning of a language to be the learning of a practice and not of a set of correspondence; he considers the speaker's knowledge of his native language to consist in the implicit knowledge of the condition under which the sentences of the language are assertible (a sort of recognition ability); but he rejects the physicalist identification of asserting with uttering, or with uttering plus a particular schedule of conditioning or a particular casual history. Rather, he identifies knowing when a sentence is assertible with knowing when it would be justified.

The use of the word 'true' is not, on theory, a mere sign that a sentence is being 'reaffirmed', as it is on the diquotation theory. To be true is to be justified. Reference, however, is not something prior to truth; rather, knowing the conditions under which sentences are about, say, tables, are true is knowing what 'table' refers to (as on a diquotational theory of reference).Indeed this idea- that objects and reference arise out of discourse rather than being prior to discourse- is rather widespread in twentieth- century philosophy, in both analytical and 'continental' varieties. (Gadamer, for example, speaks of objects as 'emerging' from discourse.)

# TRUTH AS JUSTIFICATION.

The formula 'truth is justification' is misleading in a number of ways, however, which is why I have avoided it in my own writings, in spite of the inspiration I received from Dummett's work. For one thing it suggests something which Dummett indeed believes and I do not (see 'Reference and truth'): that one can specify in an effective way what the justification conditions for all the sentences of a natural language are. Secondly, it suggests something on which Dummett's writings is rather ambiguous; that there is such a thing as conclusive justification, even in the case of empirical sentences.

My own view (for which I have suggested the name 'internal realism') is that truth to be identified with justification in the sense of idealized justification, as opposed to justification- on-present evidence. Sometimes this seems to be Dummett's view too (at such times he speaks of a 'gap between justification and truth'); at other times he writes as if ordinary-language- sentences about material objects outside theoretical science could be conclusively verified.

Consider the sentence 'There is a chair in my office right now. 'Under sufficiently good epistemic conditions any normal person could verify this, with sufficiently epistemic conditions might, for example, consist in one having good vision, being in my office now with light on, Etc. There is no single general rule or universal method for knowing what conditions are better or worse for justifying an arbitrary empirical judgment.

On this view (mine), then, truth (idealized justification) is as vague, interest relative, and context sensitive as we are. The 'truth conditions' for an arbitrary sentence are not survey able in Dummett's sense. I reject 'meaning theories.

If truth conditions and assertibility conditions are not survey able, how do we learn from them? We learn from them just the way Dummett thinks, at least in this case of the less theoretical parts of the language, by acquiring a practice. What Dummett misses, in my view, is what we acquire is not a knowledge that can be applied as if it were an algorithm. We do learn that in certain circumstances we are supposed to accept 'There is a chair in front of me' (normally). But we are expected to use our heads. We can refuse to accept' There is a chair in front of me' even when it looks to us exactly as if there is a chair in front of us, if our general intelligence screams 'override'. The impossibility (in practice at least) of formalizing the assertibility conditions for arbitrary sentences is just the impossibility of formalizing general intelligence itself.

If assertibility (in the sense of warranted assertibilty) is not formalizable, idealized warranted asseribility (truth) is even less so, for the notion of better and worse epistemic conditions (for a particular judgement) upon which it depends is revisable as our empirical knowledge increases. That it is, nevertheless, a meaningful notion; that there are better and worse epistemic conditions for most judgments, and a fact of the matter as to what the verdict would be if the conditions were sufficiently good, a verdict to which options would 'converge' if we were reasonable, is the heart of my own 'realism'. It is a kind of realism, and I mean it to be human kind of realism, a belief that there is a fact of the matter as to what is rightly assertible for us, as opposed to what is right assertible from the God's eye view so dear to the classical metaphysical realist. (On this, see 'Reflections on Goodman's Ways of Worldmaking'.)

REALISM AND REASON, Philosophical Papers Volume 3 / HILARY PUTNAM, Walter Beverly Pearson Professor of Mathematical Logic, Harvard University, Press Syndicate of the University of Cambridge The Pitt Building, Trumpington Street, Cambridge CB2 IRP 32 East 57th Street, New York, NY 10022, USA 296 Beaconsfield Parade, Middle Park, Melbourne 3206, Australia pg. xvi – pg. xviii

# ENTREPRENEURSHIP
## Spotting a Future Entrepreneur

As I researched, interviewed, my idea of what an "entrepreneur" is evolved. For the purpose of this book, an entrepreneur is anyone who starts something, who comes up with an idea and makes it real, who translates a passion into a project. This means that entrepreneurs, in my view, are not just founders of for-profit businesses, but also people who start nonprofit organizations and "profit for purpose" that are changing lives. Entrepreneurs are actors who organize their own production crews. They're musicians who put together band and find a manager and a music publisher and an agent. They're activists working to create a better world.

How con you tell if the student or the individual is entrepreneurial mind set there's no sure give away, but there are some signs to look for such as.

- Your son is a terrific student, but none of his classes excite him as much as something he does after school.
- Your daughter would rather work on her computer or paint or sing.
- The individual or son or daughter enjoys taking charge and loves organizing things or the events of people.
- The individual is always questioning why thing are done in a certain way, and they always thinking of new ways to do them.

- The individual would rather spend ten hours doing something he loves than one hour doing something he's not interested in; and even if he has trouble concentrating on  homework, or some project he's working on, when he's doing what he likes he works with great focus intensity.
- The Individual likes starting his or her own little businesses.
- Individuals are mind set to these sporting events and are focused on the outcomes of these events, and competitions.

Even if you don't think you have budding entrepreneur sitting at the breakfast table, you might be surprised. And that's a judgement call proceed with asking questions and find out who that person really is and never underestimate who a person really is until you know the true identity of the person, and what there really about.

And that's another reason it's so important to keep the path open. In most case you won't know who that person is until you take the initiative to find out for yourself.

It can be hard not to direct the individual's professional future, at least general terms. Won't making sure the person or individual succeeds at what he's attempting to do and encouraged him by building him up and by making him feel good about himself and which will have a good self-esteem, which is important for leading them to future success? Actually, the opposite may be more likely. Shouldn't the person be pushed to excel in school? Not necessarily.

So, do you have any influences over what the individual will become? Over the course of sixty thriving entrepreneurs, and I found that the answer is a resounding yes. You do have the power, just maybe not in the ways you expect.

MARGOT MACHOL BISNOW, Foreword by ELLYIOTT BISNOW and AUSTIN BISNOW, RAISING an ENTREPRENEUR 10 RULES for NURTURING RISK TAKERS, PROBLEM SOLVERS, and CHANGE MAKERS pg.4 par.4 - pg.6

# WHAT MATTERS MOST

I can't claim that every thriving, engaged, motivated entrepreneur in the world were raised by there parents who followed the same rules. But all of the extraordinary entrepreneurs I talked to did share the same core experience growing up: all of them felt truly supported.

Every individual I talked to adored his or her kids, and every Entrepreneur I talked to adored his or her mom. "The entrepreneur said thing like, "My family was always there for me." Or, "I always knew if I needed my family, they were there, which gave me the strength to take risks." Even in families where parents worked all the time, or became ill, the children new they were there when it counted.

Without my asking most of the entrepreneurs told me how important their family was to them, many also told me that they've incorporated the values their families imparted into their companies or organizations- things like trust not overreacting to mistakes, empowering employees to make decisions, and telling coworkers not to be afraid to fail.

Every one of the families in the book did a fantastic job raising confident, caring successful people. And every one of the entrepreneurs could always lean in with there families. In some cases, that meant the family provided practical or financial support. It meant no matter what, the entrepreneurs knew their families believed in them. That's what gave them the confidence to take risks.

All of the entrepreneurs in this book are extremely confident. Some may think, "Sure, success will do that." I believe that their confidence led to their success, rather than other way around. It isn't the kind of confidence that's built on a false sense of self-esteem that came from being praised regardless of whether they succeeded. It's a deep-rooted confidence that comes from realizing that they have mastered something, that stems from working really hard and gotten really good. And it was a precursor of their success as entrepreneurs. They knew do it, so they did.

When an individual trying to get a grade changed or for the coach to give them more playing time. They mean well. But the unintended effects of the individual who isn't believing that they can accomplish anything or "Master" something, that the individual can further their accomplishments or can succeed at and is not the individual's efforts that has made the difference. And that if the Individual fails, the individual can work harder and smarter and try again, because the person may succeed the next time, he or she tries if they don't their families and the ones who care about them will continue to be apart of and be proud of their success and for everything they do or whatever they pursue.

MARGOT MACHOL BISNOW, Foreword by ELLIOTT BISNOW and AUSTIN BISNOW, RAISING an ENTREPRENEUR 10 RULES for NURTURING RISK TAKERS, PROBLEM SOLVERS, and CHANGE MAKERS pg.267 par.2 – pg.269

# GOALS

When people other than yourself accomplish anything in life, your attitude has to be this; They proved that it can be done. Further, it proves that it can be done by almost anyone.

Most successful people aren't exceptional or extraordinary. I wouldn't say that I am exceptional extraordinary. Most successful people are ordinary people executing ordinary success habits and principles extraordinary well. The execution is what must be extraordinary in achieving success.

You don't have to invent Facebook or design a Telsa to be successful. You can be a teacher and be extremely successful people who living out their lives in the manner that they have decided in advance to live them out.

Observe others for inspiration, for clues on the pathway to success. Be keen observer of both success and failure because they are both good teachers.

We will all be used in comparison by others. Comparison is an inevitable happening of life. We will all be in either in the example column or in the warning column. Being the example column mean "Do what this person has done to achieve success," The warning column, of column, of course, means do what this person's done because it leads to failure and brokenness."

We want to use comparison for encouragement and to stretch ourselves and our goals to think bigger. We all can accomplish more than we typically believe. The true questions in thinking bigger are these: Why do you want it? How important is it to you? What are you willing to trade to acquire it? What price are you willing to pay?

The Black hole that's easy to fall into is not being clear about what you want. Our society rewards the beautiful people who have the outward appearance of beauty and wealth. According to the American Society of Plastic surgeons, there are 7,430 board- certified plastic surgeons in the United States. They did 17.5 million cosmetic procedures last year. That's a whole lot of beauty enhancement. Enhancing your visual image may be one of your goals. If it makes you feel better and it's truly one of your goals (not an attempt to keep up with others), Then that is a worthy goal for you.

I've admitted I have fallen into the comparison trap of houses, wealth lifestyle, and cars many times and changed my goals to keep up with the joneseses. It's easy to do in our consumer – oriented, more-is-better society. My best advice is to create your plan and work on your plan. Use comparisons to encourage you to what is possible, and don't use it as a scorecard or where you are in competition with others.

Dirk Zeller Success Habits for Dummies a Wiley Brand pg.136 par.4 – pg. 137

# MOTIVATION
## What Motivates You?
## Personal Satisfaction: The Four Cs

For smaller enterprises, sole proprietorships or businesses in which one or two key members of management have primary control, issues of personal satisfaction can be a central element in determining long term success. Some businesses fail, and other don't do as well, because their founder's owners, or key managers are uncertain what they really want to achieve or because they did not structure the company and their responsibilities in ways that satisfy their personal needs and ambitions.

It's useful to evaluate and consider your personal goals when deciding on the nature of your business development. For most entrepreneurs, these goals can be summed up by the Four Cs: Control, Challenge, Creativity, and Cash.

### Control

How much control you need to exercise on a day to day basis influences how large your company can be. If you prefer to be involved in every business decision or are uncomfortable delegating or sharing authority, your business should be designed to stay small. Likewise, if you need a great deal of control over your time (because of family or personal demands), a smaller business without rapid expansion it's more appropriate.

In a large company, you will have less immediate control over many decisions- making. Structure your management reporting systems to ensure that as the company grows, you continue to give your personal satisfaction. If you are seeking outside funding, understand the nature of control your funders will have and be certain you are comfortable with these arrangements.

## Challenge

If you are starting or expanding a business, your solver and risk taker. Enjoying the task of figuring out solutions to problems to or devising new undertakings.

It's important to recognize the extent of your need for new challenges and develop positive means to meet this need, especially once your company is established and the initial challenge of starting a company is met. Other, you may find yourself continually starting new projects that divert attention from your company's overall goals. As you plan your company, establish personal goals that provide you with sufficient stimulation, while also advancing the growth of your business.

## Creativity

Entrepreneurs want to leave their mark. Their companies are not only a means of making a living, but away of creating something that bears their stamp. That's why many businesses carry the founder's name.

Creativity comes in many forms, for some, it is the creativity involved with designing or making a new "Thing"- a fashion designer creating a line of clothes, a software developer writing a new program, a real estate delves-opera erecting a new building. For other, it may be the creativity of coming up with a new business process. Creativity also comes into play in finding new ways to make sales handle customer, or reward employees.

If you have a high need for creativity, make certain you remain involved in the creative process as your company develops. You'll want to shape business so it's not just an instrument for earning an income but also a mechanism for maintaining creative stimulation and making larger contribution to society. But don't over personalize your company, especially if it is large. Always allow room for other particularly partners and key personnel, to share in the creative process.

## Cash

Understand how your personal financial goals have an impact on your business plan. For instances, if you require substantial current income, you may need investor, so you have sufficient cash to carry you through the lean start up time. This means you will share ownership interest with others, and the business must be devised for substantial profit potential to reward those investors appropriately.

Likewise, if your aim is to build a very large company and accumulate substantial income or wealth quickly, you will need outside investors to finance such rapid development or expansion. Once again, this means giving up more control over your company.

If, on the other hand, your current income needs are less demanding or your overall financial goals more modest, you may be able to forego giving up a piece of your company to investors and instead expand your business more slowly through sales or through loans or credit lines. Keep in mind there is sometimes a trade- off between personal goals: Wanting more cash often means having less control.

(Rhonda Abrams, Planning Shop / 7th Edition Successful Business Plan Secrets & Stratigies pg. 13 - pg.15

# SELF ESTEEM

You listen to the critic because it is very rewarding to do so. Incredible as it seems, the critic helps you meet certain basic needs and listening to his vicious attacks can be reinforcing. But how can so much pain be reinforcing? How can attacking yourself be the least bit pleasurable or help satisfy your needs?

The first step to understanding the function of your critic is to recognize that everyone has certain basic needs. Everyone needs to feel.

- secure and unafraid
- effective and competent in the world
- accepted by parents and significant by others
- a sense of worth and okay-ness in most situations

People with adequate self-esteem tends to have very different strategies for meeting these needs than people with low self- esteem. If you have adequate self-esteem, you also have a degree of confidence in yourself. You keep yourself secure by confronting or eliminating things that frighten you. You solve problems instead of worrying about them, and you find ways to make people respond to positively to you. You cope directly with interpersonal conflicts rather than wait for them to pass. Conversely low self-esteem robs you of confidence, you don't feel as able to cope with anxiety, interpersonal problems, or challenging risks. Life is more painful because you don't feel as effective, and it's hard to face the anxiety involved in making things change.

This is where the critic comes in. People with low self -esteem often rely on the critic to help them cope with feelings of anxiety, helplessness, rejection, and inadequacy. Paradoxically, while the critic is beating you up, he is also making you feel better. This is why it's so hard to get rid of the critic, He can play a crucial role in making you safer and more comfortable in the world. Unfortunately, the price you pay for the critic's support is very high and further undermines your sense of worth. But you are reinforced to keep listening because every time the critic pipes up, you feel a little less anxious, less incompetent, less powerless, or less vulnerable to others.

To understand how the critic's painful attacks can be reinforcing, it's necessary to first examine how reinforcement shapes your behavior and your thinking.

Positive reinforcement occurs when a rewarding event follows a particular behavior and results in an increase in the future and the likelihood of that behavior. If your wife gives you a warm hug and thank-you after you've cut the lawn, she is positively reinforcing your gardening activities. If the boss praises the clean, spare writing behavior she prefers. Because affection and praise are such powerful rewards, you are likely to repeat your gardening and writing behaviors in the future.

Just as with physical behavior, the frequency of cognitive behavior (thoughts) can also be increased through positive reinforcement. If you feel aroused following a particular sexual fantasy, you are quite likely to conjure up that fantasy again. Thinking critically of others can be reinforced by increasing feelings of worth. Daydreams of an upcoming vacation, if they are followed by a sense of excitement and anticipation, will be repeated. The increased feeling of worth that follows your memories of success and achievement makes you more likely to return to them. Obsessing about the misfortunes of someone you dislike can be reinforced by feelings of pleasure or vindication.

Negative reinforcement can only occur when you are in physical or psychological pain. Any behavior that succeeds in stopping the pain is reinforced and is therefore more likely to occur when you feel similar pain in the future. For example, when students are preparing for final exams, they often find that most boring, mundane activities have become irresistibly interesting. In search letting you mind Concore or by finishing a certain project to know the project is completed and finished relieves a lot of high stress and anxiety will be reinforced. Anger is often reinforced by the immediate drop in tension following a blow up. Tv watching, eating, hot baths, withdrawal, complaining, hobbies, and sports activities may all the time be reinforced by tension or anxiety reduction. Blaming others relieves anxiety over your mistakes and can be reinforced until it becomes very high frequency behavior. Macho behavior has the effect of relieving social anxiety for some men and decrease in anxiety is so rewarding that the Macho style becomes a heavy armor in which they become trapped.

As with positive reinforcement, negative reinforcement shapes how you think. Any thought that relieves feelings of anxiety, guilt, hopelessness, or inadequacy will be reinforced, suppose for example, that you feel anxious every time you visit your judgmental father-in-law. Driving over to his house one day, you begin thinking about what a bigot he really is, how few of his opinions are supported by anything resembling a fact, and how tyrannical he is when crossed. Suddenly you feel more angry than anxious, and you experience a strange sense of relief. Since your critical thoughts are reinforced by reduced anxiety, you notice on subsequent visits an increasingly judgmental attitude toward the old man.

A person who feels anxious about mistakes at work may find that devaluing the job (it's idiot work) and the boss (a nitpicking, anal type) reduces anxiety. It's likely that the devaluing thoughts will be entertained again if anxiety should reappear. Felling's of helplessness can sometimes be relieved by romantic fantasies, grandiose success fantasies, rescue or escape dreams, or simply problem-solving thoughts. In every case, the particular cognition that succeeds in reducing the sense of hopelessness will be remembered. When the same feelings recur, the same recognition has a high probability of being used again.

The mourning process is a classic example of the power of negative reinforcement. What makes people keep dredging up painful memories of the lost person or object? Why keep thinking and thinking about those sweet days that can never come again? Paradoxically, these obsessive ruminations about the loss have the power of relieving pain. The awareness of a loss creates high levels of physical and emotional tension. The frustration and helplessness build until they must be discharged. Calling up specific images and memories of the lost person or object discharge the tension in the form of tears and then a brief sort of numberless. The stage in mourning of obsessive remembering is therefore reinforced by tension reduction and a few moments of relative peace.

In summary, negative reinforcement is basically a problem- solving process. You're in pain you want to feel better. You keep searching for some action or thought that is analgesic. When you find a thought or behavior that works to decrease the pain, you file it away as successful solution to a particular problem. When problem recurs, you will return again and again to your proven coping strategy.

Mathew McKay, PHD., Patrick Fanning/Self-Esteem Fourth Edition A Proven Program of Cognitive Techniques for Assessing, Improving & Maintaining Your Self-Esteem pg.23 par.2 - pg.26

# DEVELOPING HABITS AND CHARACTERISTICS THAT ARE WELCOMING

## LISTENING

The best way to be welcoming is to smile, A warm friendly smile can thaw out even the chilliest conditions.

Be genuinely curious about people, their interests, and life experiences. The hardest thing in conversation for some people to stay curious about whomever they are talking with. Most of the time, they are thinking about what to say, or they're waiting for a pause in the conversation to express their views. Be a good listener. Don't just listen for the break in the conversation. Earnestly listen to the speaker at the moment. If you catch yourself thinking about your response, then your ears might be listening, but your brain is not hearing.

One of the keys to effective listening is to encourage others to talk. The best way to accomplish that is to ask questions. Most people believe that whoever is speaking is controlling the conversation. The opposite is actually true. Whoever asks the questions is actually the guider or controller of the conversation.

Most people believe that the smooth-talking, fast-talking salesperson will have the highest sales, What if I'm not a salesperson? Well, it doesn't matter how you earn your living. The truth is, whether you are a doctor, dentist, administrative staff member, manager, student, or parent, you actually in sales. Earl Nightingale, the "Dean" of the motivational speaking industry said, "you will be successful in life based on the ability to sell." He didn't say salespeople will be successful in life based on their ability to sell, which is logical. He said you, as in all of us. I believe Earl is brilliantly spot on.

No matter your vocation or relationship in life, the ability to sell your ideas to other is imperative.

I have been in sales successfully for 30 year. My toughest pitches involve selling to my children the principles of behavior along with cleaning their room, making their bed, and picking up after themselves. And then I have to sell them on doing their homework, handing it in on time, and respecting their parents and siblings. The essence of a successful life with successful habits is effective sales skills. We are all trying to sell something to someone. If you prefer, you can substitute the word persuasion if you are challenged by world sales.

The most skilled and high earning professionals are effective in persuading people to their recommendations and points of view. I watched my father do this countless time as a dentist. In his era of dentistry, the gold standard of permanent dental procedure was a gold crown instead of an amalgam filling. The amalgam filling was about 10 percent the costs of the gold crown. The out-of-pocket cost, because only a portion of the gold crown was covered on most insurance plans, was even higher. My dad could 'sell" you on his philosophy of exceptional dentistry. He believed in doing once and doing it right. He was so persuasive that you were happy to pay additional cost for the permanent solution to a painful uncomfortable problem. I personally have a gold crown or two that he installed in my late 20s. Because of the quality of the workmanship, they are still going strong after 30 years. They will likely outlast me. You will be successful in life based on your ability to sell!

Dirk Zeller Success Habits for Dummies a Wiley Brand pg. 159 par.3 – pg.160

# COMMUNICATION

We want it to be known were sometime motivation and drive is not enough there are a few key things that we should follow and take a good understanding to for are success and to be a part of.

Communication always be neat and clean person and have a good perception or way about you to the person you are communicating with Alloway's be friendly and helpful to someone and the different situations that you will be faced with or up against nonverbal cues or verbal cues are important in communication. It's Allways's important not to hold back when communicating lean in be a part of and Alloway's have good eye contact show the person that you are talking to them!, and not someone else lets them know they are more important and be reflective express and will gain general acceptance and gain a person's trust is made with- in by a person you believe in or someone you can trust usually has for the best results rather than someone you are not sure of or you don't think you can trust. When communicating shaking someone's hand give a good handshake as opposed to not so good handshake, to show for greeting and general acceptance and familiarity and it is very important from that point on it lets that somebody know that you are on the same page as they are. Give a glance over to the people or the person and let them know you didn't forget about them.

## The Importance of Nonverbal Communication.

Nonverbal communication conveys authenticity more effectively than words do. It's good to know that a patient will forgive a poor choice of words if the caregiver takes a moment to pause and is present with authentic body language. Truth be told, I have said many stupid things that were quickly forgiven because my nonverbal communications were compassionate and super-seeded my words. Indeed, communication experts tell us that nonverbal cues carry more than four times the weight of verbal messages. Although the average person may command a vocabulary of 30,000-60,000 words, we humans rely on 750,000 nonverbal signals, Not only that, scientists have found that we interpret nonverbal signals much more quickly and accurately than words Because this kind of communication is so prevalent and significant, in order to make a meaningful connection, caregivers must attend to and practice gestures that create resonance with another person and allow meaningful conversation to evolve.

The way people walk, sit, smile, and even hold their bodies can convey innumerable unconscious messages that either prompt a conversation or stop it cold. Imagine the difference in attentiveness caregivers can telegraph by keeping their bodies still as compared to impatiently tapping a foot or twiddling a pen. In fact, investigations have shown that if physicians sit down and get on the same level as their patients, the latter perceive that their doctors have spent much more time with them than actually spent twice as much time but were standing with hand on the doorknob. They also perceived their doctor as more compassionate when they also perceived their doctor as more compassionate when they also perceived their doctor as more compassionate when they came down to their same body position.

Research has even affirmed that simply the way people stand can have an effect on their body's chemistry and how they face challenges. Psychologists Dana Carney, Amy J. C. Cuddy, and Andy J. Yap tested this by comparing participants they'd placed in assertive poses, the kind of nonverbal communication you'd see in the boardroom, with those taking submissive stances, the kind you'd see in a doctors waiting room. When they tested samples of the participants' saliva, they found that stances of power raise the level of testosterone and ultimately increased risk-taking behaviors, while at the same time lowering the stress hormone cortisol. Their findings suggest that the way people hold themselves can change the way they feel and act, in part by influencing the hormones their bodies make/ certainly, posture can affect how people relate to one another.

Important silences flushed or pale cheeks, abrupt changes of topic, or even momentary tears that are quickly blinked away they are key indicators that all is not what it seems. If after asking a woman how many children she has, she answers joylessly, "Oh, two," as she gulps and her face reddens, those nonverbal cues must be heeded and probed. This kind of attention renders caregivers' active listeners who hear unspoken problem; And, with patience and kindness, out pour a tragic story of miscarriages and still birth or a child lost to illness or accident.

In this chapter, I present research about many aspects of nonverbal communication, including the effect of facial expression and direct eye contact, how posture can communicate good intentions, the power of touch and the way gestures can reflect interest and affirmation. I also discuss techniques of posture, positioning, and mirroring that can help caregivers make a strong connection with the person they seek to help. Ultimately, they want to avoid showing the other person a "closed position", such as crossed arms, unintentional displays of boredom, or frustration. They want their physical presence to say, I'm fully open to what you have to say. And they also want to comprehend what the other person is conveying with his body as well as his words.

But before I drive in, I want to explain some of the subtitles of nonverbal communication to watch for.

# UNDERSTANDING WHAT WE'RE SEEING

It has been said that body language is the unspoken truth," But people must judge specific gestures in context. For instance, crossed arms could mean that an individual is being defensive, that he disagrees, or that he's feeling insecure. But it can also mean his arms are comfortable in this position, or maybe he's cold. Caregivers must consider what else is happening in an interaction to truly make sense of what they're seeing

This means that individuals gestures are significant only when considered within context of a person's overall behavior. If verbal and nonverbal messages convey the same information, the communication is clear. A woman says she's happy: Her eyes light up, she smiles broadly, and she walks with a springy step- no problem. But when she says, "I'm fine," yet her sad eyes, shuffling gait, and dropping her shoulders tell a different story, caregivers must pay attention to the latter. Even in the situation I observed at the hospital, although my colleague spoke kindly and sincerely to Marcie, because of his crossed arms and relative distance from her, I was unsure how his patient had received what he was saying. Unless nonverbal communication, words, and voice tone match, caregivers will be sending. Mixed messages that can confuse and ultimately distance them from the person they want to help

Besides individuals are quite adept at discerning what others really mean when they attempt to mask their feelings. People betray themselves with a thousand microscopic, unconscious clues. A finger to the side of the nose (Bill Clinton during the impeachment proceedings) or casting the eyes to the left if someone is right-handed ( is this why untrustworthy people are called "shifty" Characters?) or speaking too loudly- can all indicate that someone is being less than truthful. Real emotions are likely to leak out despites one's best efforts.

If caregivers try to deceive the person they wish to help, by telling him he looks terrific when there nonverbal cues indicate that they are worried ( being aware of the seriousness of the diagnosis, the patient is apt to mistrust them since he will resonate most strongly to the wrinkling forehead and downturned mouth, not to the words. Even if caregivers try to display a " brave front to cheer up someone," the person will recognize the insincerity, which can easily break a connection, This is all the more valid if caregivers attempt to hide from someone the true gravity of his situation with statements such as " Oh, you'll be fine" or "Next Year, this will all seem like a bad dream." Most people read what's really going... and others' attempts to smooth over the rough edges only serves to make them feel more alone, potentially activating the nocebo effect- the harm that occurs when a negative mind- set can be damaging if the interaction is inauthentic.

Whenever appropriate, caregivers must be congruent in their messages, sending the same information with their words and bodies. But what do those bodies say? And what about the bodies of the people they are charged with helping? Although it's impossible within the scope of this book to explore every nonverbal gesture, I will take a closer look at a few that can help caregivers make or ruin a good connection.

# WHAT'S IN A FACE

In the Winter's Tale, Shakespeare wrote, "I saw his heart in his face." When people first meet, they scan each other's faces for about three seconds to learn what they can- which is a lot. Studies have suggested that the human face is capable of seven thousand expressions (some have calculated as many as ten thousand), and when people interact, every countenance they make conveys there innermost thoughts, When caregivers initiate a compassionate conversation, their interest and openness show first and foremost on their faces.

These expressions are understood the world over. Facial signs of pleasure, despair, and rage are no different among Australian aborigines than ranchers in Montana or fisherman in Norway. Charles Darwin made this observation as long ago as 1872, after having collected input from missionaries who worked with native populations, individuals who were hypnotized, babies, people who were blind at birth, and those with mental illnesses, At that time, he postulated that all humans convey particular emotions with the same expressions. For instance, they usually show surprise by raising their eyebrows. People who were born blind and who there- fore couldn't observe others, still raised eyebrows when astonished.

A stony, inexpensive face conveys that one is in command and powerful. Other facial expressions are the most immediately readable indicators the people are tender and nonjudgmental, as an extension of the pause, caregivers can relax any tension in there facial muscles to show they're ready to be responsive and prepared to pay attention, When they smile kindly and genuinely in greeting another person, they begin to build a connection. But they must control their expressions beyond that first moment. A furrowed brow, scowl, or pursed lips, for instance, may suggest preoccupation with other issues, or that they are already applying prejudgments. Darting eyes may send a message that they're waiting for something more to happen, A relaxed expressions, however, says that they've dismissed other issues flitting through their minds. In addition, calmness in a facial expression says caregivers aren't about to impose their own agenda on the conversation. They're going to allow it to flow where it needs to go, with their faces, they've opened the opportunity for relatedness to begin.

However, paying attention to facial expressions can be particularly challenging in today's electronic environment. If caregivers are buried in their smartphones, or even just to stop check e-mails and text during a conversation, they've taken their eyes and attention off the other person's face and thereby broken the connection. Moreover, when inputting information on patients' computerized records, physicians and others on medical team devote much of their attention to the screen, not to the people they're helping. That to which we give attention grows! So, it behooves caregivers to become mindful of how their bodies convey their intentions and concerns.

**The Eyes.**

One of my medical students failed an exam during which students interviewed mock patients to see how well they communicated, showed Empathy, and developed trust. As he spoke with an older patient. Tom stubbornly avoided making eye contact. In his culture (Hmong), as in many others, it's a sign of disrespect to look an elder in the eye. But Tom's evaluation was based on unspoken rules of our culture, and his demeanor was found to be deficient. According to the Western way of thinking, averting the eyes indicates a lack of connection and empathy. I worked with him on this aspect of nonverbal communication, retaining how he had been conditioned as a child, and eventually he passed this test. I'm happy to say that he became a successful resident.

Eye contact is quite complex and a key element of nonverbal communication. Forty different eyebrow positions express human feelings, as do twenty-three eyelid positions. (Imagine the many permutations that exist if we multiply these numbers together.) People can enhance a good connection when they maintain eye contact about 60-70 percent of the time. But that's just the average. If caregivers are good listeners, they make contact 80 percent of the time, but only needed to do so 40 percent if there're the one doing the talking. Indeed, frequent eye contact conveys sincerity. Ninety percent of the glances focuses on the triangle created by the eyes and mouth.

Where people place their glances is also important. Rolling the eyes upward is unsettling and can indicate disinterest. Or contempt. Downcast eyes can convey sadness or shame. If the person one wishes to help doesn't maintain eye contact but maybe rejecting the caregiver or what he is saying. The eyes of anxious or stressed people involuntarily blink more often than those who are not so upset. Although the former may make eye contact as often as people who are less stressed, they hold the glances for less time. This especially true of people who are depressed. They maintain eye contact only 25 percent as long as people are not depressed. At the same time, as Tom, my Hmong student, learned the hard way, those whom caregivers wanted to help may interpret minimal eye contact as a sign of stress or a negative response.

Even the pupils in the eyes matter. When they dilate, they indicate that people are seeing or experiencing something pleasurable, which they want to take in. The pupils dilate to let in more light, the more light the more they want to see. Conversely, when the pupil's contract, it means people are dealing with some unpleasantness that they'd rather shut out. These reactions are entirely unconscious, yet they can still help caregivers understand someone's frame of mind. Indeed, this is why poker players wear sunglasses when they're at the table. The shades keep the other players from seeing the subtle pupil dilation that might reveal the winning hand.

A small gesture as it is may be, caregivers can convey many feelings with their eyes, including caring and compassion. In our culture, meeting another person's gaze and being willing to maintain eye contact (but not staring, which means hostility) begins building trust. It may seem merely like, as simple as greeting an individual by name, but in fact, these are acting that people remember.

**The Smile.**

Along with eye contact, smiles also convey what people are thinking. A smile reinforces friendliness, disarms a difficult situation, and promotes peace and safety- all to the good. I mentioned smiling kindly upon greeting someone, but often people also smile when they are uneasy or even anxious. Ethnologist Fran de Waal explains in peacemaking among primates that young rhesus monkeys grin when they're feeling threatened. "In social situations," de Waal writes, "the grin signals sub mission and fear; it is the most reliable indicator of low status among rhesus monkeys. In other species, such as humans and apes, this facial expression has evolved into the smile, a sign of appeasement and affiliation, although an element of nervousness remains." Think of the third-grade teacher yelling, "And wipe that grin off your face!" after she finished reprimanding a student.

Authentic (or Duchenne)smiles are controlled by major facial muscles that connect to the corners of the mouth (the zygomaticus major) and the area encircling the eyes 9the orbicularis oculi). According to Guillaume Benjamin Amand Duchenne, the French neurologist who first published these discoveries in 1862, when these eye muscles contract, the cheeks lift, the skin under the lower eyelid's puckers, and wrinkles appear at the outer corners of the eyes. This is a genuine smile. However, at a party or other social gathering, individuals can (and often do) fashion their mouths into a broad, fake smile at will, even if they're feeling unhappy or angry.

Indeed, in our culture people especially those who are depressed or sad- will hide their true feelings by smiling. When observed sharply, one might detect a false smile because the eyebrows, eyes, and forehead don't move much. That's where to look to really understand a person's emotional state.

The crinkling of the muscles around the eyes (creating crow's feet) when people truly smile is unconscious and it's hard to be willed into existence. Most people can distinguish a false from genuine smile. The latter lights up the face and eyes, indicating enjoyment, while the former shows mostly on the mouth and is more likely to be perceived as an attempt at deception. Before considering Botox injections to erase crow's feet, people should remember that those wrinkles inform others of their sincerity and genuine pleasure, without them, faces appear too plastic and are unable to convey one's true emotional state.

Delivering bad news may render clinicians anxious. However, softening the blow with a false smile can send a mixed message that's both confusing and off-putting. So, it's helpful for caregivers to be mindful of their smiles if they find themselves in this difficult situation. Otherwise, the connection they're trying so hard to build may rupture for reasons that may feel mysterious to them.

# HAND AND ARM GESTURES

People may begin an encounter with a handshake, witch in bygone time revealed a weaponless hand, and remains in many cultures a sign of respect and mutual agreement. A compassionate handshake generally involves a firm grip that convey confidence 9one's own self-respect will respect back to the individual) but isn't arrogantly strong or overbearing. It's softened with kind eyes. A tender addition to the handshake may be a touch with the left hand on the other person's right elbow or covering their right hand with one's left during the encounter. These signals of warmth at the right moment can be as welcoming as a smile. The dominate person usually takes the top position during a handshake. If caregivers want the client to feel more confident, it's easy to roll to roll their hand under so the client's hand is on top. But ideally both hands are equally vertical.

Caregivers should observe the resting hands of the person they wanted to help. If they lay limp and floppy in her lap, she may be sad or have low self-esteem. Fidgetiness or grasping behaviors can show anxiety, as can shakiness or twitching. The white knuckles of a clenched fist can conceal anxiety or anger. But palms turned up out can denote warmth and openness.

The patients may use her hands to indicate that she wants to interject her ideas into a conversation. To do so, she may create a steeple in front of her face by touching the tips of her fingers to each other. Steepling suggests that she has something important to say and can signify self-assurance. Or she may raise her hand or simply an index finger slightly to indicate that she wants to speak. On the other hand, if she places the same finger on her lips (as if to says!"), she may be trying to keep her ideas to herself. In that case, a caregiver may want to probe a bit further to see what's on her mind, or he may to explain himself more clearly.

If someone has folded her arms, she may be signaling a "closed" attitude. In effect, her arms are creating a physical barrier to the situation or information she's receiving. People also use this stance when they're bored or expectant or are braced for displeasure. Some people say crossed arms, "I just do it because it's comfortable" But as evident in conversation between Marcie and her physician, the nonverbal cue can also communicate. I am not fully open to what you have to say. However, if a person's arms are so tightly crossed that she seems to be hugging herself, she may be feeling insecure or sad and could benefit from being comforted.

# POSITION.

When people are seated, they signal their interest an engagement by sitting tall and learning just a little bit forward. On the other hand, leaning back can make them seem less interested and even complement. Sitting rigidly erect indicates tension also not the best position to take when making a connection. And too much of forward angle can seem aggressive- as if someone were encroaching in an overbearing way. Personal space differs by culture. In the United States, it is two to three feet- basically an arm's length. Length. For other it is much tighter. Caregivers should not move closer to someone than what's acceptable until they're invited into the other person's space, even when seated.

In addition, when caregivers initiate a compassionate conversation, they must make sure they are positioned at a similar level to the person they're caring for. Seating arrangements that place one person higher than the other can suggest the presence of hierarchy or privileges a can instantly be off-putting. For instance, if a doctor is standing, conducting the conversation while looking down on a patient who is sitting or stretched on an examination table, the patient may feel diminished. It's hardly away to make a person empowered.

Similarly, a parent who wants an honest answer from his teenager about whether drinking is taking place at parties would do well to sit down with their teen face-to-face. Having a conversation on the same physical plane doesn't make the father and child peers- there's still an imbalance of responsibility and authority- but the physical position helps ease a dynamic of blamefulness and defensiveness, enabling a more productive conversation to ensure.

# TOUCH.

Some experts in nonverbal communication consider touch to be the master sense-underlying all others. Think about it. We taste something when it touches our tongue, hear something when sound waves touch our ear drums, and see something when images touch are retinas. Indeed, touch has been called the most influential nonverbal communicator of all. It can change the meaning of words almost instantly, even if the utterance seems unimportant.

Beneath awareness, the skin can send and receive information that is quite important. One research study showed that waitresses who touched their customers for than a second on the shoulder or hand when returning change or the credit card slip received larger tips than those who refrained from physical contact with their customers. In another investigation, students whom college librarians grazed briefly on the hand at checkout rated the quality of the library much more highly than a control group that received no such touch. And many studies of preterm babies in the NICU who are held skin to skin on the parent's chest and gently stroked clearly establish that these infants need fewer interventions, recover much more quickly from the effects of their prematurity, and leave the hospital sooner.

When touched is included in the medical encounter, patients perceive them appoints as longer and more positive than they actually are. If I'm in a hurry and the situation does not demand a long visit, I will still try to incorporate touch into the therapeutic ritual. This is why the physical exam is so important, even if I feel the presenting complaint doesn't warrant it.

While other cultures may condone frequent cheek kissing, hand-holding, and hugging, in the United States there are many unspoken rules about when and where to make contact. Touch communicates a wide spectrum of feelings from antagonism and anger to comfort and love, and the same behavior can have many meanings depending on context, duration, and intensity; the toucher's intent; and where on the body the contact occurs. For instance, it would be perfectly acceptable for mother to tuck her young son's shirttails, but she would be awfully upset is a stranger attempted this to tidy him up in this way.

Many professionals touch the people with whom they interact with every single day- say a nurse or manicurist or dental hygienist. This has been called "cold touch" since in most instances, not much emotion is conveyed. These individuals are simply doing their jobs, which involve physical contact. Shaking a colleague's hand or tapping a woman on the arm to indicate that her purse has opened or that the bank teller is ready to receive her as called social-polite touching. People do this all the time with acquaintances. It's relatively anonymous, in contrast to touch that indicates friendship and warmth. That's when a person puts an arm around a friend, hugs, or otherwise physically reassures someone's close to them. The most intense kinds of touch involve intimacy and love- caressing, kissing, holding, cuddling. These behaviors soothe, bring comfort, and elicit the release of oxytocin.

As a physician, I am required to touch my patients, palpating an abdomen or feeling around the throat for the thyroid gland, for example, when I perform a physical. But also, consciously touch them when I listen to their hearts. In one hand, I hold a stethoscope to their chest, but I place the other on their back, creating a type of hug. This is much more than just listening to the heart. I'm taking them into my hands and conveying that I am there to support and care for them.

If caregivers are not in an intimate relationship with someone but still want to offer a reassuring or comforting touch while helping them, the safest spots are on the outside edges of their body; the back shoulder, outside of the arm or leg (when seated). And although helpers may believe that everyone needs a hug, it's important to note that hugs don't Allways's heal. Some people feel uncomfortable with close physical contact. Pushing it on them can undermine trust and connection. Or they may have some medical reason that would obviate a squeeze. I learned this out the hard wat when I hugged a colleague who, it turns out, had severe arthritis in her shoulders. My friendly embrace caused her to undue her pain. It's the best to learn about the person's unique situation and ask if it's all right to hug before making a move.

# MIRRORING

When synchronizing two engines, one changes its speed to come into rhythm with the other. The same can be true of the brain. Perhaps due to mirror neurons, two people can fall into step with each other, mimicking each other's feelings and nonverbal signs. Not all of this is unconscious. "Body mirroring" is a behavior that can be learned. In fact, many business books provide chapters on how and when to do this. Everyone from the CEO to salespeople are familiar with using their bodies to win over potential clients. I can assure you that drug reps are quite adept at this. The idea is to take the other person's nonverbal communication- without calling attention to the gestures in order to convey respect and establish trust.

Ultimately, earning "respect" in sales gets someone to buy what salespeople are selling. But in the compassionate encounter, caregivers mirror nonverbal communication to put patients at ease and to show that they are ready to meet them where they are. If the patient slouches, the caregiver might partially slouch too His slouch says, "I see you're low, and I feel your pain."

When mirroring in this way, the caregiver's body helps create res or resonance or rapport with the other person; it's an important wat to forge a connection

Clinicians can also lead or guide with their own bodies to help someone open up and share valuable information. They start by mirroring a patient's body language and developing trust with the eyes subtle caring expressions on the face. Then, once the connection is started, they slowly unfold their bodies to a more open position in hopes that the other person will follow suit. Here is how this might work; If the patient is sitting in a closed position- for example, arms folded over the chest and legs crossed- the caregiver would imitate his stance. Next, the caregiver would model a more relaxed version of this position with loosely crossed arms and legs. This posture is less defensive and indicates availability. Then, the caregiver would uncross his or her legs entirely and lean forward to show engagement. Finally, the patient's new openness would telegraph that he is uncomfortable and ready to share.

Nonverbal communication is not simply a mirror but part of an evolving yet subtle dance. Caregivers hope their bodies prompt in the speaker that fundamental instinct that, yes, the conversation feels right, and that any words yet to be spoken will be well received.

On the other hand, when the patient moves in such a way that he disrupts the mirrored position, he may be indicating discomfort, disagreement, or sense of betrayal that he can't (or won't) put into words. If caregivers notice this disconnect, it would be wise to address what might have prompted it.

# HOW TO TELL WHETHER SOMEONE IS LYING.

Other nonverbal behavior communicates that an Individual is shading the truth or outright lying. For instance. I might ask a patient whether he is ready to stop smoking. He may tell me that he is. But his nonverbal cues indicate that he isn't. I can deduct this even before he answers because he has used what's called respiratory avoidance response. He coughs as if to clear something from his throat even though there's nothing there. This behavior generally suggest that he is uncomfortable with what he's saying.

Or he may put his finger to his nose the way Johnny Carson, one of our early hosts of the tonight show. Used to do before telling a risqué joke. This is not vigorous rub a person would use to scratch an itchy nose but a few gentle strokes or flicks. Some experts believe this is "a reflection of the fact that a split is being forced between inner thoughts and outward action." As mentioned earlier, while Bill Clinton testified before a grand jury, he touched his nose in frequently when he was truthful, but he did so twenty-six times when he lied. Someone who tugs an earlobe, scratches the side of his neck, rubs one eye, blinks to excess, or smiles for too long (most natural smiles last four or five seconds) can also be stifling his emotions or shading the truth.

If caregivers notice these behaviors accompanying a "fine!" in answer to their question, "How are you doing?" or "tell me more."

# PUTTING IT ALL TOGETHER.

A patient's first contact with his or her caregivers is key. It is where the patient will perceive whom the caregivers are and whether they will be a good fit. The interactions following that first impression- one that can be led to a strong connection. For instance, caregivers should read the patients energy and react in a way that shows respect. If someone engages, they should convey a message through the eyes that they are available and have their full attention. If appropriate, caregivers can touch the patient in some way. This is generally a handshake, but it also may be a gentle touch on the shoulder. They should mirror the patient's body language and then slowly lead him or her to an open and trust position, as indicated above.

The pause should be utilized appropriately if caregivers note an emotion that warrants further exploration. For instance, the patient's eyes slightly roll up when asked when asked about marriages, caregivers should stop, show concern, and gently pursue the emotion with a question such as. "when I asked about your relationship, I saw that a tear came to your eye" {… pause} or "If that one tear could speak, what would it want to say?" In this regard, it's important to watch for consistency between body language and words. If there is a disparity, gently explore further.

If a patient doesn't participate in the therapeutic dance (he or she doesn't partake in mirroring, for instance), caregivers should not force the issue, as this will upset the individual. Rather, with words and nonverbal cues, they can show caring, and perhaps the person will be more open the next time they meet.

When someone is willing to partake in the dance of connection, enjoy it! This is one of the most rewarding interactions caregivers can have. And once two people connect, it creates a chemical reaction. Both are transformed.

David Rakel / Golant Susan K, The Compassionate Connection: the healing power of empathy and mindful listening / David Rakel MD, with Susan K, Golant, MA. pg. 166 par. 2 – pg. 186

# IT ENABLED BUSINESS TRENDS
# FOR THE DECADE AHEAD

The social matrix also extends beyond networks we examined in our 2010 article more business conducted distributed problem-solving trapping brain powers of customers and experts from with- in and outside of the company for breaking through thinking. (Boehringer Ingelheim) Kaggle- (A platform for data analysis contest) new drug molecule would cause genetic mutations

### Global IT Service Supplier Atos

2014 aiming to boost employee's productivity by replacing internal email with social networking and platforming.

Europe (RTL) Group- Social Media for feedback such as x factor, RTL to finetune episode Plato.

### Competing with 'Big Data' And Advanced Analytics

Experiments with segments consumer markets using big data. As with Social Matrix, we now see data analytics a part of a new foundation for completeness.

Data Volume surging from Social Web, Sensors, Smartphones and more-are double faster every two year. The power of analytics is rising while cost is falling. Data visualization wireless communication, and cloud infrastructure are extending the power and reach of Information corporate spending allowance, Corporate Capabilities, Retirement.

### Deploying the Internet of All Thing

New technologies are leading to what's as the quantified self-movement, allowing people to become highly involved with health care by using devices that monitor blood pressure and activity- even sleep patterns. Providing new opportunities to manage health and disease

### Offering Anything as A Service

Moves like this will suggest that cloud delivered It can be reliable and resilient create new possibilities for the provision of mission critical IT through internal or external assets and suppliers. It has a range of companies transforming them into services benefiting corporate buyers that can sidestep owning them.

And a growing number of companies with excess office space are finding that they can generate revenue buy offering space for short term uses. Other companies are seizing opportunities in consumer markets.

IT that can track usage and bill for services Is what makes models possible.

### Automating knowledge Work

Physical labor and transactional task have been widely automated over the last three decades. Now advanced in data analytics, low cost computer power machine learning and interface that 'Understand' humans are moving rapidly toward the world's more than 200 million knowledge workers powerful productivity- enhancing technologies already taking root. Allowing computers to search for new information and find patterns of meaning at superhuman speeds.

### Engaging the Next Three Billion Digital Citizens

In dividing tradition mom and pop stores and multinational adapt products for business models to local conditions. The devices relay information (such as stock level and pricing) back to companies, so unclever can improve its demand forecasts, inventory management and marketing strategy- Rising sales rural stores by a third.

### Charting Experiences with Digital Media

The boarders of digital and physical world have been burning for many years as consumers learn to shop in virtual stores and to meet virtual spaces in through case online mirrors expressions of the physical world.

Increasingly were seeing a version as real-life activities, from shopping to factory work, become rich with digital information and as mobile internet these advantages in natural users' interfaces and gives the physical world digital characteristics. Today's app usage of smart phones and technology to sense over locations and thoughts of our friends or even us to allow us to point to foreign street signs for quick translation. Google is in part a reality in the next generation deploys wireless cameras and wireless connections and other areas of demand. Information on demand. Other valuable technologies were finding out about steam from intelligent textures to wristwatches and computers that runs mobile apps and tex. Because you are also integrating the digital world into physical work activities. There by boosting their productivity and effectiveness and effectiveness. Boeing uses virtual glasses so that factory workers assembling it's 747 aircraft need to construct manuals less frequently innovated pop-ups points to drilling locations and display proper wire connections.

Executives need to examine their persuasiveness to find areas where immersive experiences or interactive touch point can stimulate engagement with 'Alloway's on customers. And they should reflect on the potential for interactive digital platforms to play role in product design and marketing or in gathering customers feedback. These importance's as customers and employees come to expect interaction between heightened digital and physical offerings.

## Freeing Your Business Model Through Internet

Inspired personalization and simplification after two decades of shopping, reading watching, seeking information, and interaction on the internet customers expect services to be free personalized, and easy to use without instructions. This ethos presents a challenge for business since customers expect results as well. As superior and transparent customer service for all interaction from web sites to brick and motor stores fail to deliver and competitors offering an app two download away. Consumers, meanwhile, expect to be valued by companies and treated as individuals. In the online world Spotify and Netflix analyze their customers histories to create for me experiences when recommending music and movies. Services are becoming even more hassle free online new web and mobile apps are designed to be easy to use that institution are now longer needed the demand for quick and easy is competing companies to modify how they delivered real work offerings for example pay allowing customer to photograph checks and deposit them using smartphone app award of digitalized instant gratification and low switching costs could force many businesses In motivated business models that provide more products and services free of charge or at lower costs they also have to think about offering more personalization in their products and services customization at mass levels, this approach could require changes to back end systems, which are often designed for mass production business will need new ways to collect information that furthers personalization to embed experimentation into products developments and efforts, and to ensure that offerings are easy to use and even fun.

# BUYING AND SEEKING AS DIGITAL COMMERCE LEAPS AHEAD

As the rise of mobile internet and evolutions of core technologies that cut cost and vastly simplify the process of completing transaction online are reading barriers to entry across a wide world of economics activity amped-up technology platforms are enabling peer to peer commerce to replace activities traditionally carried out by companies and given birth to new kinds of payment systems and motivation models Starbucks envisions extending its powering use of smart phones for payments to unglue instant photo verification of buyers (GDP) Growth.

# TRANSFORMING GOVERNMENT, HEALTHCARE AND EDUCATION

The private sector has a big stake in the successful transformation of government, Health Care and Education witch to get the account for a third global (GDP). They have fallen behind in productivity growth at least in part because they have been slow to adopt Web- Based Platforms, Big Data Analytics and other IT Innovations. Technologies- enabled productivity growth could help reduce the cost burden while improving the quality of services and outcomes as, as well as boosting long term global growth prospects finally there is education witch represents 4.5 percent of global (GDP) immersive math course ware dream box makes learning more final while Algorithms adapt the learning experience to each student's needs. Brilliant.org allows talented mathematician and physics students around the world to learn at the Owen pace. Global massive online open courses (Moocs) offer university level "Classes using social networks, videos and community interaction. Smartphones and Tablets are entering the classroom end mass to deliver personalized content. India is running trials of the sub- $50 Aakash tablet to make a little more than 25,000 colleges in an E learning programs. Other technologies are improving teachers' skills and performance through online collaboration to access to the best in class pedology's and better tracking of student's achievements, which facilitates targeted in interventions.

Transparent and Innovation business models. Real time information instant price discovery and quickly problem resolution are becoming basic expectations of consumers citizens and business customers in digital realm. Collectively they will force many companies to rethink elements of their business models, leaders will need to make their companies more transparent and elevate rapid responsiveness to the level of a core competency. Business models built on transparency and responsiveness will not only satisfy customers but also help companies become nimbler innovated, and credible with all their stockholders.

Organization the Internet model and values particularly connectivity and notifier article interactions, have significant organizational implications. The flowering of many of these trends could imply decentralization along with changing relationships among managers, changing relationships among managers, employees, suppliers and customers these shifts are not always comfortable for leaders but they told the potential for boosting innovated loyalty business reach Productivity, Marketing, Effectiveness, while reducing costs.

# FINANCIAL STRATIGIES

Directly related to your Financial Strategy is your sales structure- how you achieve actual customer orders. In this section of your plan, described for two main components of your sales system: The sales force and the sales process.

If your business plan document is being used for external funding requests, you don't need to go into detail; it's enough to provide a general outline, giving essence of your understanding of what is necessary to produce sales, For internal planning, however, you should put into context more thoroughly and base it on Financial Importance's.

**Accounts payable.** Obligations owed to others; others list of outstanding bills.

**Accounts receivable.** Obligations owed to your company by others; a list of outstanding invoices.

**Accumulated Depreciation.** The amount of depreciation a company has already taken in the form of tax deductions; such accumulated depreciation must be accounted for when selling fixed assets.

**Assets.** Anything the company owns having a positive monetary value.

**Cash.** Immediately available money in form of currency, checks, or bank deposits.

**Cost of goods.** Expenses directly associated with producing and making a specific product. Companies differ as to which expenses attribute to cost of goods, but generally includes more indirect labor, and freight are included.

**Cost of sales.** Expenses directly with selling a product or service. This typically includes item such as sales commissions distributors' fee, and so on, but does not generally include more indirect costs such as marketing.

**Current assets.** Assets that can be converted quickly with relative case, to cash; these assets are designed to be turned over in the normal course of doing business, such as bank deposits, inventory and accounts receivable.

**Current Liabilities.** Any bills, debts, or obligations occurring in the ongoing course of business; any debit due with-in the next year. Includes accounts payable, accrued payroll expenses, and loans and credit lines with less than one-year maturity date.

**Debit.** An ongoing obligation of the company, such as a bank loan.

**Depreciation.** The wear and tear on fixed assets- not cash expenditures, but an ongoing expense of the business as equipment wears down, as a Tax deduction.

**Equity.** Ownership of a company usually distributed by means of shares of stock. A person who owns part of a company is said to have equity interest in the company

**Exchange rate.** The price at which one currency is converted to be received in another currency, for example, if 100 US dollars are worth 120 Australian dollars, the exchange rate 1.2 and if 100 US dollars are worth 80 euros, the exchange rate is 0.8.

**Fixed assets** (or property, plant, and equipment). Assets are the ongoing means of doing business; such assets are generally cumbersome to turn into cash; includes buildings, land, and equipment.

**Fixed cost.** Ongoing expenses or overhead of a business that occur regardless of the amount of sales. These expenses usually include items such as rent, utilities, and salaries.

**Gross profit.** Percentage of income your company realizes on each sale before administrative expenses.

**Liabilities.** Any outstanding obligations or debt of the company.

**Long-term liabilities.** Loans and other debts that come due in more than one year's time. This year's interest payments on such loans, or debt service, are included in Current Liabilities

**Net profit.** Amount of income deducting all costs of doing business, including administrative overhead and other fixed costs.

**Net worth.** Value of a company after deducting liabilities from assets.

**Other or intangible assets.** Aspects of your company that have value not easily interpreted in specific monetary terms or directly convertible to cash; assets such as a popular trademarked name and the Goodwill a company has built up over time.

**Profit.** Amount a company earns after expenses. Pro Forma. Financial statements based on projected future performance rather than actual historical data.

**Retained earnings.** Net worth amount the company keeps internally for ongoing development of the business rather than distributing to share holder.

Ronda Abrams: planning shop/ 7th edition successful business plan secrets & strategies pg. 180 par.2

Rhonda Abrams: planning shop/ 7th edition successful business plan secrets & strategies pg.298 - pg.299

# REFERENCE PAGE.

Jacques Bughin – How the EU scale up artificial intelligence? A minute with MGI's Jacques Bughin, Mckinsey Company Feb. 8, 2019 YouTube:

Jacques Bughin – Technology and the future – Dr. Jacques Bughin CEDA news Sept. 25, 2017

Jacques Bughin – ITU telecom world 2018: Jacques Bughin ITU YouTube – Sept. 11, 2018

Edx – IT Support: Communications – If you are interested in pursuing a career in IT support, this course examines how to improve your basic customer communication skills.

Edx – Student's Text and Homework Matrix and "Big Data"

Edx – David Christopher Platt Micro Master of Business program, M.B.A.

Alzay Calhoun – Coveted Consultant- What Does Your Client Really Want.8

Alzay Calhoun – Coveted Consultant- Consulting Purposal: Why you should not use them.

Alzay Calhoun – Coveted Consultant- How to find consulting clients

American Bandstand: Dick Clark and the making of a rock 'n' roll empire/ John A. Jackson pg. 57 par.4

# AUTHOR.

My name is David Christopher Platt born on Canada Day and received a Medallion on July 1, 1967 in Montreal, Canada in the province of Quebec popular for their fine foods and fine French cuisine and Aubon coffee croissants and pastries all known for and very well. The language fluently spoke in the province of Quebec is French Canadian not to far away from the hospital were I was born is the French Quarter were they speak fluent French and shops and businesses are there for window shopping or if you want to go in and look around a lot of time being in a clean city like Montreal, Canada and the atmosphere of the French Canadian people, That's makes it all worth the while to get out and get some clean and fresh air and get some shopping done.

Artwork is very popular different Mosaic trends to look for. If I do say its eye catchy and it's very much fashionable and really a beautiful place. And enjoy the fine atmosphere and the French-Canadian people, the fine French cuisine they have to offer.

Very popular back then the TV show American Band Stand with TV's Host Dick Clark moving up the Billboard Carts and getting the ratings back in 1957. Bringing in a large Black American crowd and the idolizing of Rock n Roll music from the 50's.

Another popular seller was a book called One Night in Paris.

Me and my family are all out of New York, my mom Frances Platt is from Spring Valley, New York, and my father Calvin Platt is from Monsey, New York. Then moved from them to upstate New York to the town of

Washingtonville, New York and lived in a nice family house a pleasant atmosphere and a country type of living outside the BIG city.

Then ventured out to Colorado we lived in Lakewood, Colorado were I went to school there through my first year in high school played intramural sports in school one year are Baseball team almost went to the Nationals in Farmington, New Mexico but are team came in 2$^{nd}$ place to a tough Denver Team. A lot of good talent some of them advanced and moved on to play semi- pro Baseball, Basketball, Football, and other sports.

Then after 10 years the family would move back to New York were our family is from and we were renting are house out at this time and live the countryside living of upstate New York.

That was ok for awhile and then decided to head down south to sunny South Florida, were we live in the suburb outside the city over 30 year's now, it's nice the weather's nice, and if there's a place to take care of business and get work done, it would have to be there. An Entrepreneurs paradise a great place if your getting education or working on an internship, then Florida is a good place to be.

www.ingramcontent.com/pod-product-compliance
Lightning Source LLC
Chambersburg PA
CBHW051535170526
45165CB00002B/736